Learnin

'*Learning Whiteness* is a defiant corrective to the attempts to deny the existence of systemic racism. Examining the ways in which whiteness is taught, learned and normalised in educational institutions, Sriprakash, Rudolph and Gerrard confront relationships between the field of education and the workings of modern settler colonial states that remain deeply invested in racial hierarchies and practices. Refusing the lure of easy "solutions", they argue that education has an ongoing responsibility to open up spaces for grappling with racial injustice and imagining futures freed from racial domination.'

—Professor Paul Warmington, author of *Black British Intellectuals and Education*

'*Learning Whiteness* is a much-needed analysis of education for teachers, policy makers and activists interested in racial justice. This book serves as an important reminder that all schools within the colony operate on the sovereign land of Indigenous People, whose rights to land and self-determination have never been ceded. Readers are challenged to confront the colonial foundations of schooling, and the violence this has brought along with the strength of those resisting such violence, so as to rethink equitable education futures.'

—Hayley McQuire, co-founder and CEO of the National Indigenous Youth Education Coalition, Australia

'The field of race and whiteness studies in education receives a fresh and bold update in *Learning Whiteness*. Decisively structural in their analysis, resolutely critical in their orientation, and radical in their hopes, Sriprakash, Rudolph and Gerrard centre the white settler state in educators' understanding of why schooling assumes its form in modern western societies. Unsettling this multidimensional and historical formation requires a sustained and careful examination, which this book delivers and commands our attention. In an already crowded field like race and whiteness studies in and out of education, the authors manage to stoke our anti-racist imagination about the possibilities of a world after whiteness. A welcome addition to any institutional or personal library on the topic of race and racism.'

—Professor Zeus Leonardo, University of California, Berkeley, author of *Race, Whiteness and Education*

'*Learning Whiteness* offers a compelling, incisive and authoritative analysis of Australian settler colonialism and its impact on marginalised communities. This is a defiant and timely contribution to the field. It carefully exposes the oppressive contours of whiteness which is all the more essential in an era marked by the heightened surveillance and attempted eradication of racial justice pedagogies.'

—Professor Nicola Rollock, King's College London

'In this theoretically astute book, the authors provide the reader with the coordinates to make sense of whiteness' ongoing creation, its reactions to perceived threat, and how education is a crucial extension of the state in settler colonial structures. Through rich examples and careful theorising, we are offered both a comprehensive and accessible guide to confronting the desires of whiteness. As James Baldwin wrote long ago, we cannot change our realities if we don't understand them. This book offers that understanding; it is crucial for a long overdue unsettling of whiteness.'

—Professor Leigh Patel, University of Pittsburgh, author of *No Study Without Struggle*

'This is a book of highly impressive scholarship, critically reflecting on an issue that has long troubled scholars but has now become politically urgent. The question of how racism associated with white privilege is learned is of vital importance in contemporary settler societies in which new abstruse forms of racism are emerging which are increasingly difficult to name, let alone tackle. This book provides a most perceptive and insightful analysis of this difficult question in ways that are not only theoretically astute and accessible but also pedagogically helpful.'

—Fazal Rizvi, Emeritus Professor, University of Melbourne, and University of Illinois at Urbana-Champaign, author of *Globalization and Education*

'*Learning Whiteness* opens important and troubling questions. Settler colonialism is an economic and political structure based on dispossession, that generates racism and continuing injustice. Is "education" the answer? Arathi Sriprakash, Sophie Rudolph and Jessica Gerrard, highlighting Indigenous scholarship, trace how the education systems created in settler-colonial history have actually sustained white privilege, and do that in multiple ways. To change this is no small task; it requires a deep re-thinking of institutions, ideas and practices.'

—Raewyn Connell, Professor Emerita, University of Sydney, author of *Southern Theory*

'*Learning Whiteness* provides rich conceptual resources for critically comprehending how education is shaped by and extends racial social orders in colonised and colonising societies. The authors work importantly towards imagining an education that enables reparative rather than racially dominant futures.'

—Professor David Theo Goldberg, University of California, Irvine, author of *The Racial State*

'While many works argue that whiteness is constructed, very few go into the actual process of construction. This book does. It takes us to the educational construction site where the white mind-body assemblage is fashioned. This makes for an important addition to the literature on whiteness.'

—Professor Ghassan Hage, University of Melbourne, author of *White Nation*

Learning Whiteness

Education and the Settler Colonial State

Arathi Sriprakash, Sophie Rudolph and Jessica Gerrard

First published 2022 by Pluto Press
New Wing, Somerset House, Strand, London WC2R 1LA

www.plutobooks.com

British Library Cataloguing in Publication Data
A catalogue record for this book is available from the British Library

ISBN 978 0 7453 4214 6 Hardback
ISBN 978 0 7453 4215 3 Paperback
ISBN 978 1 786808 61 5 PDF
ISBN 978 1 786808 62 2 EPUB

This book is printed on paper suitable for recycling and made from fully managed and sustained forest sources. Logging, pulping and manufacturing processes are expected to conform to the environmental standards of the country of origin.

Typeset by Stanford DTP Services, Northampton, England

Simultaneously printed in the United Kingdom and United States of America

Contents

Acknowledgements

This book is the outcome of long-term collaboration, not just between the three of us, but also with the many communities of practice we each care for and learn with. It has also been written on shifting ground. Changing discourses of racism in education fruitfully challenged our thinking, and the vicissitudes of our lives conditioned our writing: lockdowns and making new homes, children and new relationships, unmanageable workloads and strikes. And, of course, our everyday encounters with whiteness. This required us, at times, to put down the books we were reading and the drafts we were writing. But, if these were 'interruptive' moments, they also helped us to see the importance of sustaining our conversations, picking up the ideas again, and recognising that our learning for this project is (still) not complete.

Research and writing for this book took place, in part, on the lands of the Wurundjeri-Woiwurrung people – land that has never been ceded. We acknowledge Aboriginal and Torres Strait Islander people as First Nations people of what is now known as Australia, and pay our respect to elders past, present and emerging. We work in academic institutions which sit on stolen land in Australia and in the heart of Empire in England, and which are, in different ways, complicit in sustaining the project of whiteness. We came to writing this book to reckon with these tensions, to consider how the very idea and practice of education that we ourselves are enmeshed in can be fundamentally remade. We are grateful to many people who supported this endeavour; whose encouragement, challenge and critique helped us refine our arguments. Particular thanks go to Leon Tikly, Zeus Leonardo, Licho López López and Derron Wallace for their invaluable feedback on early writing and presentations. Some of our thinking for this book has been published in the journal *Race, Ethnicity and Education* (Gerrard, J., Sriprakash, A., Rudolph, S. 2021. Education and Racial Capitalism) and we are grateful to Taylor and Francis (https://www.tandfonline.com) for permission to elaborate on these ideas in the pages that follow.

Arathi would like to thank the Race, Empire and Education Research Collective (REE). REE offered me a nourishing intellectual space and a refuge from the debilitating racism of my former department at the University of Cambridge. Many of the ideas in this book have been inspired by and enriched through REE reading groups over the last five years. I am so grateful to learn alongside each and every member of the collective and for the opportunity to continue our conversations through this book. I would also like to thank communities within my new institutional home at the University of Bristol. Focused study with the Memory, History and Reparative Futures group has been enlivening, and meeting new colleagues at the Centre for Comparative and International Research in Education offered warmth in the darkness of the pandemic. The generosity and guidance of friends, colleagues, students and family have helped shape this book in ways that many will not know. Mónica Moreno Figueroa, Hettie Malcomson, Sharon Walker, Kevin Myers, Julia Paulson, Angeline Barrett, Fazal Rizvi, Leon Tikly, Tigist Grieve, Derron Wallace, Keri Facer, Rafael Mitchell, Robin Shields, Jenny Gibson, Paulina Sliwa, Tyler Denmead, Sarah Fraser, the Knowle Park and Redcatch crews, among many others – thank you. Scott and Lekha, your support and joy sustains me. Through all the uncertainties of the world, my love for you is always.

Sophie would like to thank the various networks of scholars, practitioners and activists who inspire me, keep me accountable, challenge me and contribute to imagining better ways of living together in this world. These include: the Justice-involved Young People Network, the National Indigenous Youth Education Coalition, the Koorie Youth Council, the Social Transformations and Education Academic group at the Melbourne Graduate School of Education (MGSE), the Indigenous Curriculum Taskforce at MGSE and the Melbourne Educators for Social and Environmental Justice. There have been many people I have had conversations with about the work we are doing in this book – which have helped to push and sharpen our ideas as they developed – and who have offered support through the writing process, including: Melitta Hogarth, Stephen Chatelier, Kate O'Connor, Beth Marsden, Archie Thomas, Mati Keynes, Rosie Barron, Marie Brennan, Lew Zipin, Sanmati Verma, Fazal Rizvi, Annabel Meagher, Isabelle Rudolph, Sianon Daley, Jessica Gannaway, Rosie Welch, Sarah Truman, Eve

Mayes and Jane Kenway. And to family, friends and comrades who bring joy, light and laughter to my life, thank you.

Jessica is grateful for her supportive network of collaborators and colleagues. To the members of (and 'friends of') Social Transformation and Education, I am so appreciative of being surrounded by such a generous group of colleagues and students within MGSE. Thanks must also go to the many collaborators on the MGSE Indigenous Curriculum Taskforce; finding and forging spaces to rethink and rework knowledge within the institution has been sustaining (even with its challenges!), and I have learned so much from you all. Across these groups at MGSE, particular mention must go to Melitta Hogarth, Liz McKinley, Julie McLeod, Fazal Rizvi, Lyn Yates and Sarah Truman. In addition, over the time of writing this book, I have been immensely grateful for the many meaningful and supportive research and writing collaborations. The thinking, laughing and writing across all of these projects have supported me in this book: thank you Glenn Savage, Helen Proctor, Sue Goodwin, Jessica Holloway, David Farrugia, Steve Threadgold, Chris McCaw, Anna Hogan, Elisa De Gregorio, Rosie Barron and Juliet Watson. Thanks too to the 2020 posthuman reading group – our Zoom discussions were like a little glimmery light in the midst of the seemingly endless Melbourne lockdown. And finally, thanks to Manda, Indigo and Aster, whose love, life and giggles soothe even the worst of writing days.

Together, we'd also like to express our gratitude to Sharmilla Beezmohun for carefully editing our manuscript and to Neda Tehrani and the team at Pluto Press for supporting this project.

Arathi Sriprakash, Sophie Rudolph, Jessica Gerrard
Bristol and Melbourne
September 2021

PART I

WHITENESS: PAST, PRESENT, FUTURES

I
Educating the Settler Colony

> In school, they told me Captain Cook was a hero and discovered Australia. It made me confused. It's not true because before cars, buildings and houses there were just Aboriginal people. I want Australia to tell the truth that Aboriginal people were the first people who had the land.
>
> Dujuan Hoosan, twelve years old, Arrernte and Garrwa Country, Speech to the United Nations, 2019[1]

> ... education is the first defence of the nation. It is critical to our prosperity, harmony and advancement as a country.
>
> Josh Frydenberg, Treasurer, Australian government, 2019[2]

We begin this book with two quotes which, when read together, reveal the tensions at the heart of education in the Australian settler colony. Josh Frydenberg, the Federal Treasurer, conjures a militaristic image of education: fending off threats and keeping a nation strong; being a line of defence. But he also invokes education as critical to the prosperity, harmony and advancement of the country. How such prosperity, harmony and advancement is achieved through education is, however, deeply disputed. Dujuan Hoosan, a young Indigenous person from Arrernte and Garrwa Country, made this clear in his recent speech to the United Nations.[3] He asks that schools in Australia teach the truths about the nation that have been actively kept from students for centuries. These two comments show how education has been used to defend and fortify the settler colonial state against the fact that First Nations people have never ceded sovereignty. Dujuan's statement ruptures the force of the dominant white settler colony that Frydenberg's comments attempt to uphold. To reinforce its authority, settler colonialism requires the active and continual defence of white domination. This is what we explore as learning whiteness. Whiteness, in this sense, is an ongoing educative project and its lessons are constitutive of the settler colonial state.

We have called this book *Learning Whiteness* to shine a light on the fact that systems of white domination are not predetermined or natural, rather they are forged and sustained through specific and ongoing practices of colonial violence and racial injustice. This is to say, whiteness is not innate, it is made and it is learned. By whiteness, we refer to the structural formations of racial domination tied to European colonialism which continue to be reinscribed across all aspects of social life, mediating understandings of self, relations with others, work within institutions, and ideas of the nation. While this book focuses specifically on learning whiteness within Australia, it offers a grounded account of the workings of British settler colonialism as a *globally* enduring project. Lessons in whiteness make and sustain global colonial and capitalist orders, seeking to normalise and relay racialised hierarchies within and across states.

Key to our thinking here has been the important work of Goenpul scholar Aileen Moreton-Robinson, especially her book *The White Possessive: Property, Power and Indigenous Sovereignty*.[4] As Moreton-Robinson argues, the unbroken sovereignty of First Nations people in settler colonies challenges the legitimacy of settler states and their 'possession' of Indigenous land.[5] This is the challenge contained in Dujuan Hoosan's words above. Because of its illegitimacy, the settler colonial state continually strives to maintain its dispossession of Indigenous people and its occupation, expropriation and ownership of Indigenous land.[6] Moreton-Robinson calls this the logic of the 'white possessive'. To maintain Australia as a white possession, the settler state must constantly work to preserve the structural formations of racial dominance. In this book, we examine how this work is facilitated through education, through learning whiteness.

Indeed, education is a key social institution; it brings together people as much as ideas – whether in the formal places we go to, for example schools or universities, or in the processes of learning that occur in other spaces, for example through media, rituals or civic participation. Across its forms, but perhaps most recognisably within its institutionalised sites, education is highly contested, generating debates over knowledge, access, equity, purpose and delivery. Education is, therefore, an enactment of ongoing politics; policy and governance regulate and circumscribe its work in the face of constant resistance, refusal, remaking and the reinvention of its practices. Across its operations, sites and processes, education is informed and mediated by social, cultural and political values and aspirations. In *Learning Whiteness* we focus our attention on the specific ways in which the political normativity of the settler colonial state – that is, the values and aspirations of white domination – has both shaped education and been produced through it.

Education and the settler colonial state

As Gamilaroi scholar Michelle Bishop points out, despite policy discourses seeking to 'reform' education, Australian schools are not '"broken", but, rather, operating perfectly, as they were intended: as part of an imperial agenda'.[7] Education has played a central role in cultivating and maintaining the power of whiteness in Australia and other British settler colonies, and it is through this agenda of white domination that some people benefit and others are harmed. This is to say, whiteness works differently upon different racialised groups: Indigenous; white settler or immigrant; Black or Brown immigrant, refugee or settler. It is also mediated through ableism, hetero-patriarchy and classism as simultaneous forces of domination under settler colonialism.[8] Despite its different inscriptions, whiteness works upon us all because the settler state asks – expects – *all* to participate in its lessons. Sometimes whiteness is learned so well, its lessons are so ubiquitous, that it is taken for granted; it can remain unseen by some or felt as inevitable and incontrovertible by others. To some, whiteness is seen as rightful, its lessons absorbed. For others, the wrongfulness of whiteness is recognised, even contested. Across all these relations to whiteness, its injustices, harms and violence continue to be levied upon – and also challenged by – individuals and communities.

In this book, we inspect the educative project of whiteness – how it is relayed within formal institutions such as schools and universities, as well as its lessons in public and media discourses – precisely to make visible and interrogate the 'grammars' of racism that are bound up in educating the Australian settler colony.[9] Three analytic frames are developed to explore the complex operations of learning whiteness.

These are what we call the material, epistemic and affective dimensions of education in the settler colonial state. Identifying these three dimensions allows us to look at: the racialised extractions of resources and divisions of labour that build and sustain education systems; how knowledges which challenge the legitimacy of the settler state are denied and distorted within education institutions; and the ways in which complex attachments and investments of feelings can protect and bolster the white possessive. By bringing these three dimensions together we trace how whiteness is made, known and felt through education systems and practices. Across each, we work with conceptual resources – namely, racial capitalism, epistemologies of white ignorance and feeling-states – which illuminate how whiteness is taught and learned, not only within the Australian settler colony, but also across other sites of colonialism, including within its persisting centres in Britain and Europe.

We therefore intend that this book is read as an 'entangled' or 'connected' study of whiteness and education, demonstrating the specific forms of learning whiteness in Australia but also capable of illuminating such lessons at other sites of British settler colonialism.[10] While racial injustices operate differently in different contexts, we only have to look at transnational solidarity movements to see the through-lines of domination wrought by colonialism and capitalism.[11] Indeed, the racial injustices that shape life within British settler colonies cannot be separated from the abiding power of whiteness that endures within Britain itself. We hope, then, that our interrogations of whiteness as a far-reaching structural formation can connect individual, institutional, national *and* global reckonings with racism in education.

In focusing on the educative forces of whiteness, we do not set out to story the pain of racism experienced by individual people or groups, real as it is. Turning experiences of racial injustice into 'objects' of academic inspection or intrigue can sometimes shift the analytic gaze away from the sources of oppression. Instead, we prioritise examining those very sources – the material conditions, knowledges and feelings – that create and sustain systems of white domination in and through education. Our method has been to think with a range of writing on racism, education and settler colonialism: drawing together research and arguments; re-reading work through the lens of how whiteness is learned; analysing particular historical and cultural events; and reflecting on our own experiences as settlers educated on stolen land and our differing relationships to whiteness. In this sense, the book's project of understanding how whiteness is learned has been one of reading, thinking, remembering and listening. For, as Palyku poet and academic Ambelin Kwaymullina writes,

> Listening
> means learning to hear
> the noise of settler-colonialism
> inside your head[12]

The noise of setter colonialism

We have been writing this book at a particular time in the history of the settler colony. In Australia, as around the world, we are witnessing a resurging white nationalism and white supremacist extremism that is becoming more and more mainstream.[13] Public and political discourse has formed what some have called a vocal 'ecosystem' of racism.[14] Within parliament, Australian politicians have voted for the national school curriculum to reject discussions of the systemic nature of racism, following similar attacks against Critical Race Theory in the USA and UK.[15] In the Australian media, the systemic nature of state violence against Indigenous people is repeatedly denied and distorted.[16] But this is also a time in which interconnected movements for Indigenous sovereignty, Black Lives Matter, refugee justice and anti-racism offer a different vision for the country with a clarity which has inspired a growing reckoning with the multiple forms of racial domination that structure life on stolen land.

This is not, however, an 'unprecedented' moment in time. While this book is not a 'history' of education in Australia, it nevertheless demonstrates how state violence, assumptions of white superiority and racist backlashes have been consistent features of the settler colonial state. One of our aims in writing *Learning Whiteness* is to demonstrate how contemporary recalibrations of white domination are functions of an enduring system rather than something new or newly noisy. That settler colonialism is an abiding structure, its past and present conjoined, is what allows continued state violence across the world: Aboriginal and Torres Strait Islander deaths in custody in Australia,[17] missing and murdered Aboriginal women in Canada[18] and the violent dispossession of Palestinians by Israel[19] are each expressions of racial domination fuelled by settler colonialism.

We come to the writing of this book as settlers, each of us formally educated in different parts of the vast country now known as Australia. We have learned the lessons of whiteness on the sovereign lands of the Wurundjeri-Woiwurrung, Boonwurrung, Gadigal, Durug and Larrakia peoples, in settler institutions that failed at that time even to recognise Country and the diversity of Indigenous Australia. Arathi is racialised Brown. Sophie and Jessica are racialised white. This means we have had very different experiences of the racism produced by white settler dominance. While now living in England, Arathi remembers how the racist abuse felt growing up in Australia, back in the era of supposed 'happy' multiculturalism.[20] It is deeply felt now too, in those everyday assertions of the white nation, mainstreamed and sanctioned by politicians and media, within places of work and in spaces of social life.

And yet, despite our differences, each of us – like everyone in Australia – has been invited to participate in the project of whiteness. For instance, we remember as school children being given a silver coin in 'celebration' of settler arrival (or more precisely, invasion).[21] Looking back now, we understand this glossy commemoration of settler colonialism as an active lesson in whiteness. Across our school and university education we received a purposefully selective curricula based on Eurocentric knowledge; into adulthood we are repeatedly asked to understand the carceral violence of the state as acceptable – from the off-shore detention of refugees to the systemic imprisonment of First Nations people. As former school teachers and now university lecturers and education researchers, we have each been implicated in educational projects which seek to diminish and destroy Indigenous sovereignty, knowledge, culture and history and which extend and translate such racial violence to people of colour more broadly.

We write this book, then, with a responsibility to learn and teach differently, to 'listen to the noise of settler-colonialism'. We document the constructions and workings of whiteness in the hope that the field we ourselves are enmeshed in – education research, policy and practice –

can more squarely address its material, epistemic and affective investments in systems of racial domination. As students and teachers, we have been faced with the despairing inadequacies of educational efforts to 'manage problems' which don't actually name the problem of whiteness. For, in all the policies and initiatives of multiculturalism, diversity and inclusion that spin around us, there has been a persistent failure to centre unceded and unbroken Indigenous sovereignty. This is why this book focuses unrelentingly on whiteness as a structural, but always contingent, force. Through the lens of learning whiteness we can better understand how the experiences and consequences of racial injustice are different for different people, yet interdependent and underpinned by the central problem: the logic of the white possessive.

We place emphasis on the *contingency* of whiteness here. The histories and lives of Indigenous people and people of colour are not reducible to, or defined only by, the intrusions of whiteness. There are spaces and stories that sit outside of white dominance or refuse to be captured by a settler framing of it. As Yawuru scholar Shino Konishi writes, the limitation of the settler colonial framing is that it can be conveyed as an immutable structure, teleological and deterministic in its violence, assuming totalising or fatalistic destruction, and denying the agency and 'supple and complex' connections that Indigenous people have always brought to evading its forces.[22] Konishi's careful reading of Aileen Moreton-Robinson's work, for example, shows how, even when the white possessive has attempted to 'physically remove Aboriginal people from their country, [it has] not severed Indigenous ties to land'.[23] Thus, in starting from the premise that whiteness is not innate but is learned, *Learning Whiteness* is alive to the fact that lessons in whiteness are not simply digested; they can be – and often are – resisted and refused. It is precisely the pedagogic possibility of collectively breaking the relay of whiteness that animates our analysis.

Learning and refusing the pedagogies of the state

By now we hope it is clear that this book does not take education for granted. Education – as an idea, as a practice and as an institution – is deeply implicated in the settler colonial project of racial dominance but also in its refusal and undoing.

In seeking to understand the role of various educative efforts of white dominance in the making and maintenance of the settler colonial state, we work with the idea that learning whiteness takes place through what we call the 'pedagogies of the state'. Jessica Pykett has explored the idea of the pedagogic state as entailing 'pedagogic strategies employed by the state and "non-state" agencies – both within and outside of the formal educational sphere – to govern citizens'.[24] Following Pykett, we also underline that 'pedagogies of the state' refers to interventions or lessons not only by 'state actors' but also by all those working in the interest of the white possessive of the settler colonial state. Across educational institutions, private enterprise, public and media discourse and social relationships, there are educative practices that, while not always *by* the state, are *of* and *for* it. As we discuss across Part I of this book, identifying and examining these 'teacherly' occupations offers opportunities for understanding the settler colonial state as active and invested, as an entity that is not fixed or predestined, but one formed and reshaped through ongoing relations of people and ideas.[25]

Indeed, our interest in the pedagogies of the state does not imply that the state engages in a one-way didacticism. Within the teaching of settler white dominance, there is also challenge and rescripting; the settler colonial state must deal with constant dissent, refusal and survival in its effort to expand and contain and control. A lens on pedagogy enables awareness of the tensions between domination and dissent, relay and reshaping, in all educational relationships. For example, formal education institutions of the state have been called upon by many Indigenous communities to better serve their students; First Nations truth telling is a key part of these calls as well as the teaching of a 'both ways' curriculum.[26] Moreover, while many of the discussions in this book deal with institutionalised forms of education, this is not to say that education and learning only occur in sites of 'formal' training. Drawing together histories of Black and Indigenous struggle in North America, Leigh Patel reminds us that learning in settler colonies has often taken place as a 'fugitive practice' outside, against and despite formalised education, and often through covert means. Referring to the lessons taught within Black and Indigenous homes and communities and the learning that takes place through social movements and collective action, Patel argues that learning has 'never yielded fully to [the] settler project of colonization of the mind'.[27]

A lens on pedagogy, therefore, allows us to consider the means and methods through which racial domination has been sustained and reworked in the face of resistance and refusal. That the settler colonial state is made and reshaped through these pedagogies casts education as one of the most powerful modes through which the relations of the state are formed; that is, the relations between people, knowledges, capital, land and feelings that constitute political normativity in Australia. Despite education being central to these relations, it is often overlooked within literature in the political sciences on state making and remaking. Yet, we argue that the *generational* reach of education serves well the long view – or intended permanency – of settler colonialism. Our aim, then, in drawing on the idea of the pedagogies of the state, is to document, if only partially, the active and ongoing investments of the state in whiteness as a temporal project. As we continue to discuss in the next chapter, coloniality – understood as the power of colonialism that endures across social and political life – seeks to accumulate and expand the past and present domination of whiteness in order to secure its future.

In Part II we look at the modes of learning whiteness more closely, examining its multiple operations across material, epistemic and affective dimensions. Starting with the materialities of learning whiteness, Chapter 3 considers the systems of racial capitalism underpinning institutions of education and educational priorities in the settler colony: relations of enclosure/dispossession, divided labour and extraction of value. Capitalism and racism are inextricably linked and, as we demonstrate, have been constitutive of education systems in Australia. This, we suggest, has been a key means through which whiteness is learned as 'productive' for the settler state. In Chapter 4 our discussions turn to the epistemic bases of learning whiteness, examining the knowledge that circulates through formal education institutions as well as through public discourse to sustain whiteness as the norm for understanding the world and the nation. We argue that this knowledge is not neutral or objective; it is profoundly political and, as we demonstrate, it is produced through an 'epistemology of white ignorance' that reproduces global systems of white supremacy. In Chapter 5 we take up the complex ways in which learning whiteness occurs through the affective lessons of the state. We outline how these lessons involve what we call 'feeling-states' of whiteness which actively project pride, superiority and benevolence alongside putting up defences that emerge from fear, anxiety and perceived woundedness. These are oscillating feeling-states through which the interests of whiteness are protected.

Over the three chapters of Part II we show how whiteness is learned in the Australian settler colony across each dimension, but also how each is intricately intertwined. For instance, the epistemic dimension of education – such as the kind of knowledge valued within school curricula – is tied to the material conditions of how that knowledge is produced: the racialised and extractive economies of universities. Affective attachments to whiteness are rendered material as well as sustained epistemically through, for instance, commemorative events and media discourses – allowing the ongoing violence of settler colonialism to be felt by some as benign, right or inevitable. It is these linkages that we attempt to illustrate across the chapters and that, as we suggest in Part III of the book, compel a project of reparation that stays with complexity in order to divest from whiteness.

Staying with complexity

The project of settler colonialism, which we ourselves as non-Indigenous settlers are enmeshed in, involves ongoing attempts to recuperate or recentre whiteness. Thus, across this book, we look to thoroughly reject the too-often presumed innocence of whiteness. Instead, we seek to more fully recognise and reckon with its injustice. As Torres Strait Islander scholar Martin Nakata has demonstrated through his study of the colonial constructions of Torres Strait Islanders, it is at the 'cultural interface' that Islanders make sense of individual and collective experience.[28] It is the complexity of this 'interface' that brings together multiple histories and experiences, and that enables a greater awareness of power and of how it operates in everyday lives. As Nakata and others have argued, education in the Australian context needs to attend to these complex politics of knowledge, requiring the 'suspension' of foregone conclusions, closures or resolutions that tend to push students into binary thinking, opposition or defensiveness.[29] Across our analysis, we look less to specific 'solutions' for education and instead explore how the epistemic, material and affective conditions of being educated in whiteness demand an active, systemic and collective response. In Chapter 6 we draw together these reflections to reckon with the implications of deeply knowing the work of the settler state on our lives. This requires the capacity to stay with complexities and complicities, rather than turn away from them.

The argument we advance in this book is that individuals and publics become enmeshed in, and attached to, racist colonial orders through repeated and normalised lessons in whiteness. And it is only through becoming critically and deeply aware of these multidimensional lessons that we might understand our collective and personal responsibilities to build futures free from systems of racial domination.

2
Whiteness and the Pedagogies of the State

The concept of whiteness helps illuminate the racial contours of contemporary Australia and their global connections. Perpetuating white domination has been central to how the project of British settler colonialism has made and remade itself in the face of First Nations sovereignty, ongoing histories of migration, and multicultural and multilingual polities. Whiteness is thus a structural formation, shaped by the material interests of racial domination under colonialism and capitalism, and constantly reworked and reinscribed through the governance of social and political life. To see whiteness in these material terms is also to recognise that it is steeped in settler colonial networks of social and cultural power. For example, as we explore later, there have been ongoing attempts by political, media and business elites to assert the cultural superiority of 'Western civilisation' and 'Christian heritage' as the defining and rightful educational basis of the nation, actively denigrating multifaith pluralism and First Nations sovereignty as 'faddish rubbish', 'brainwash' and 'race propaganda'.[1] Not only is whiteness a structural formation that is aggressively defended in these ways, it is also sutured into other systems of domination: capitalism, hetero-patriarchy, ableism and so on. Thus, whiteness is not outside of understandings of classed or gendered inequalities, for example, but rather central to their articulation.

To understand whiteness as a *formation* is to be alive to its mutability and contingency. What and who is considered 'white' depends on context and political power.[2] This is to say, while whiteness forms through and around people and their ideas and actions, it is not reducible to a fixed 'identity'.[3] This means there is a motility to whiteness. As David Theo Goldberg observes of the adaptability of whiteness, 'working and immigrant classes might be devalued from or promoted into the relative privileges, powers and properties associated with middle-class whiteness according to the political, economic and cultural demands and interests of place and time'.[4] People have greater or lesser proximity to whiteness, variously benefiting from or harmed by its power, inhabiting and habituated by its structures, depending on how they are racialised and how they are positioned by other systems of domination. Whiteness therefore moves through and is reshaped by political systems, institutions and daily interactions in different ways, reforming racial orders and being itself a malleable formation.[5]

We are particularly interested in how the mutability and contingency of whiteness relates to the temporal project of settler colonialism: the reformulations of racial dominance in the past and present, and the projection of whiteness into imagined futures. For, in the face of unbroken Indigenous sovereignty, the settler colonial state can only continue to have its claims of legitimacy heard by updating the structural forms of whiteness and reasserting its power. This temporal project of settler colonialism is what leads us to consider whiteness as something that is reproduced through intergenerational relay, with education a central means of remaking and sustaining white dominance in material, epistemic and affective ways. Whiteness, in this sense, is an ongoing state project; there is a self-conscious orchestration of its formations and instrumentalities in and for the settler colony.[6]

In the discussions that follow, we trace this temporal project and elaborate on our treatment of whiteness as a structural formation. We begin by situating the historical production of whiteness within the global systems of European colonialism and capitalism, and specifically in relation to the 'white possessive' of British settler colonialism.[7] This leads us to consider how the power relations of white ownership that have been central to both colonial dispossession and capitalist expansion endure, and how they create what scholars have called 'racial states'. We then explore how the power of whiteness in the Australian settler colony accumulates and expands into the present, maintaining its occupying forces and contributing to a range of contemporary expressions. In the final section of this chapter, we outline our interest in the 'pedagogies of the state': the educative means by which particular pasts and presents are claimed and relayed in order to secure the futurities of whiteness. Ultimately, it is these pedagogies of the state – the project of learning whiteness – that are the subject of this book.

The global project of racial domination

There is no scientific basis for the differentiation of people by race. However, racial thinking – specifically, the supremacy of whiteness – has emerged and persisted through the material, and globally entangled, histories of colonialism and capitalism. As Gomeroi scholar Nikki Moodie argues, it is important to begin with a threshold understanding that racial thinking – how people are hierarchically categorised in racial terms – is not natural or inevitable, but is thoroughly the expression of power.[8] That is, racial categories are produced through what a number of scholars explore as historically specific processes of 'racialisation'.[9] Furthermore, the racial categorisations of people, knowledge, resources, land and histories are not anomalies of past and present political systems but, rather, are constitutive of their modes of power. This is why racial thinking – in all its complex, multifarious forms – might be best understood as a 'technology' for making and managing systems of social domination.[10] Indeed, as Lisa Tilley and Robbie Shilliam point out, while race 'began as a fiction', it has become 'material over time', creating 'the manifold raced markets of the global political economy'.[11]

The convergence of capitalism and European colonialism in the sixteenth and seventeenth centuries gave rise to a pliable but powerful notion of race that bolstered the British colonial project of the eighteenth century, which has continued all the way into the present.[12] To draw on the opening words of Cedric Robinson's landmark text *Black Marxism*: 'The historical development of world capitalism was influenced in a most fundamental way by the particularistic forces of racism and nationalism.'[13] Robinson goes on to analyse how the tendency of European civilisation through capitalism was 'not to homogenize but to differentiate – to exaggerate regional, subcultural and dialectical differences into "racial" ones'.[14] This process of racialisation interlocked with capitalist enterprises of colonialism in the sixteenth century: 'the peoples of the Third World began to fill this expanding [racial] category of a civilization reproduced by capitalism'.[15] It was in the seventeenth and eighteenth centuries, Robinson suggests, that 'race became largely the rationalization for the domination, exploitation, and/or extermination of non-"Europeans" (including Slavs and Jews)'.[16] Thus, race was articulated into the categorisation systems of capitalism, with those deemed of 'inferior' racial status relegated to the bottom of the hierarchy to be exploited by those self-elevated as 'superior' with greater social power.

Through violent invasion of lands, exploitation and enslavement across the Americas, Africa and Australasia, European colonialism honed this hierarchy of race – producing what African American sociologist W.E.B. Du Bois famously called 'the colour line'.[17] Identifying the colour line as the defining, and global, problem of his time, Du Bois observed with clarity and directness that this was a problem of *whiteness*. In 1910, over a century before the recent explosion of the field of 'whiteness studies', Du Bois set out to inspect whiteness, asking 'what on earth is whiteness that one should so desire it?'[18] He documented its long tentacles, how it touched states, societies, beliefs and souls: 'wave upon wave, each with increasing virulence, is dashing this new religion of whiteness on the shores of our time'.[19] As historians Marilyn Lake and Henry Reynolds have reflected, Du Bois theorised whiteness as 'at once global in its power and personal in its meaning, the basis of geo-political alliances and a subjective sense of self'.[20] And, much like the analytic of 'the white possessive' put forward by Goenpul scholar Aileen Moreton-Robinson, Du Bois recognised that whiteness is, at its core, proprietorial: 'I am given to understand that whiteness is the ownership of the earth forever and ever, Amen!'[21]

The global reach and intended futurity of whiteness ('forever and ever') that Du Bois identified can be explored through the lens of what scholars working in Latin American decolonial thought have referred to as the 'coloniality of power'. Recognising that colonialism involved 'the violent concentration of the world's resources under the control and for the benefit of a small European minority – and above all, of its ruling classes', Aníbal Quijano argues it produced and continues to maintain a 'global power covering the whole planet'.[22] The concept of coloniality draws attention to this power as longstanding and entangled, but also as enduring; it has defined 'culture, labor, intersubjective relations, and knowledge production well beyond the strict limits of colonial administrations'.[23] In doing so, it resonates with Patrick Wolfe's well-known theorisations of settler colonialism as a 'structure', not merely a temporally distinct 'event'.[24] As Nelson Maldonado-Torres suggests, coloniality 'is maintained alive in books, in the criteria for academic performance, in cultural patterns, in common sense, in the self-image of peoples, in aspirations of self, and so many other aspects of our modern experience'.[25] Coloniality – and its embedded racialisations – shapes life in the modern nation-state; modernity and coloniality, in this sense, are two sides of the same coin.[26]

Indeed, the ongoing manufacture of racial thinking has been central to settler colonial states such as Australia, New Zealand, Canada and the USA, gripped as they are by the coloniality of power. As Aileen Moreton-Robinson demonstrates, foundational to the formation and management of these modern states is the perpetual disavowal of Indigenous sovereignty and the construction of the nation as a 'white possession'. Necessary to the existence of white domination – ideologically, epistemologically and ontologically – is, Moreton-Robinson suggests, the possession of Indigenous land as the '*proprietary anchor* within capitalist economies'.[27] The apparatuses of the settler state – its governments, institutions and laws – legitimate the appropriation of Indigenous lands, which are then claimed as the property of white people and institutions, governed by white laws and policies, and made productive in the service of white interests.[28] Whiteness as a structural formation, then, is made and inscribed in the settler colony through the possessive logics and instrumentalities of the state. Whiteness, as racial domination, is therefore no accident of history; its past, present and future is by design.

Racial states: white sovereignty, ownership, power

In his book *The Racial State*, David Theo Goldberg traces how the modern state is deeply and self-consciously invested in racial thinking and racial orders. The apparatuses and technologies of states have served in different ways 'to fashion, modify and reify the terms of racial expression, as well as racist exclusions and subjugations'.[29] This is to understand states not as fixed or timeless entities but, rather, as actively and continually shaped by racial interests. Indeed, as Goldberg argues, through legislative, economic, cultural and social practices of governance, states are 'instrumental in defining and refining, projecting and policing who should count in the class of the privileged, propertied, and powerful and who could not'.[30] He defines states as racial because of 'the structural position they occupy in producing and reproducing, constituting and effecting racially shaped spaces and places, groups and events, life worlds and possibilities, access and restrictions, inclusions and exclusions, concepts and modes of representation'.[31] The perpetual struggle over sovereignty drives the racial project of the settler colonial state, whereby states exercise authority not only in response to perceived external treats, but also in relation to assumed internal ones. At the heart of this struggle in Australia, both inside and outside its borders, is the anxious desire of the settler state to maintain the coloniality of its power – its whiteness.

Aileen Moreton-Robinson expands on Goldberg's work to argue that British settler colonies like Australia are foundationally 'racial states' because 'patriarchal white sovereignty' is the defining and refining condition of their formation.[32] White sovereignty and the white possessive were initially deployed by conferring legal entitlements to those categorised as white, and were then reinscribed in the twentieth century through property rights, the carceral governance of Indigenous people, and immigration and citizenship laws – such as, in Australia, the Immigration Restriction Act of 1901 (otherwise known as the White Australia policy) which severely restricted 'non-white' immigration. To this day, white sovereignty in British settler colonies continues to inform 'the legal exclusion and regulation of those who transgress within and outside its borders'.[33] Observing that this ongoing work of the racial state is often characterised as benevolent and virtuous, Moreton-Robinson explains:

> The possessive logic of patriarchal white sovereignty is compelled to deny and refuse what it cannot own – the sovereignty of the Indigenous other. This ontological disturbance/fracture is one of the reasons why the state deploys virtue when working hard at racial and gendered maintenance and domination in the guise of good government.[34]

Indeed, Ghassan Hage's now classic analysis of Australian multiculturalism and immigration policy in *White Nation* shows how, beneath the logics of both ('evil') white racists and ('good') liberal multiculturalists, there is a common assumption – the right to white ownership, mastery and control of Australia.[35] Hage argues that the settler state is 'a space structured around a White culture, where Aboriginal people and non-White "ethnics" are merely national objects to be moved or removed according to a White national will'.[36] A searing example of this assertion of white sovereignty is the deliberate and ongoing dehumanisation of asylum seekers and refugees in political and media discourse.[37] In 2001, for example, the then prime minister John Howard declared that refugees adrift on sinking boats at sea were trying to 'intimidate us' and falsely claimed that they were throwing their children overboard. Bolstering a new era of hard-line immigration policy that continues today across party lines, Howard made a muscular declaration in his re-election campaign: 'we will decide who comes to this country and the circumstances in which they come'.[38] We are reminded here of Moreton-Robinson unravelling the conceit of the white possessive: 'you cannot exclude unless you assume you already own'.[39]

Such presumptions of white possession continue today across all aspects of social life. For example, in a recent study of an institution emblematic of state governance – the Australian Public Service (the federal civil service of the Commonwealth of Australia) – Kamilaroi and Wonnarua scholar Debbie Bargallie documents the 'racial state' at work. Bargaille examines Indigenous accounts of working in the public service to show the deep, pervasive and systematic racism of the institution. These lived experiences of racism, she argues, 'do not emerge out of isolation', but are borne from the legislations, policies and administrative practices of the racial state, maintaining hierarchies of colonial power at the very centre of Australia's governing apparatus.[40] Such testimonies of racism will come as no surprise to people harmed by the structures and expressions of whiteness in the settler colony – to those who are confronted with racism in their workplaces, in their civic and social lives, in their education spaces and communities. As Moreton-Robinson argues of white sovereignty and white possession in the racial state, 'the state's assertion that it owns the land becomes part of normative behaviour, rules of interaction and social engagement embodied by its citizens'.[41]

This is what brings us to consider the racial state as 'relational'. While there are concrete expressions and practices of the state – embodied in its schools and universities, borders, laws and resources, for example – there is also a sociality to them. The state, Goldberg argues, looks to effect 'a language of mutual comprehension and deployability, and of common practice. ... People after all do not live out their economic, political, social, legal and cultural lives discretely but interactively, in interconstitutive and mutually determining terms.'[42] In other words, we are invited to learn whiteness, to deploy and practise it together. Looked at in this way, the power of the state emerges from how people relate to it, what people think it does and represents, and how people call versions of it into being through their everyday actions or political contestations. As Mohawk scholar Audra Simpson writes, 'To be *within* a state is to some extent to be *of* a state, since one must come up against its image, its history, and its law as one moves through and upon it.'[43] In this sense, we approach the 'racial state' of the Australian settler colony as deeply structured by the ongoing logics of the white possessive, but also as continually projected, claimed, made, relayed, contested, refused and experienced. Passing on lessons in whiteness – teaching and learning – is so crucial to the making of the racial state because this is how whiteness is able to accumulate, expand and endure.

Accumulating and expanding whiteness

Maintaining the conceit and authority of the white possessive relies on accumulating its power and expanding it across all aspects of life – including personal, collective, national and global relations. Michelle Christian argues that the historical accumulation of whiteness is a global phenomenon that shapes all geographies, 'but in different, nuanced and indirect forms', working across racial systems of states, economies, institutions, discourses and representations.[44] While we've spoken so far about whiteness in largely structural terms with respect to its proprietorial foundation, the accumulated power of whiteness is also deeply embodied, interpersonal and defining of selves; it is experienced, used, expressed, held on to and protected in a multitude of ways. As Cheryl Harris' field-shaping examination of 'whiteness as property' shows, racial identities, opportunities and exclusions are substantively tied to the structural formations of whiteness as a 'property interest'.[45] Both whiteness and property share the central concept of 'the right to exclude'; they condition socio-legal and economic access, participation and status.[46] And whiteness is also 'something that can be both experienced and deployed as a resource'; it contains, like property, the rights to use and enjoyment.[47] Thus, whiteness – like property – accrues status, value and reputation. Working with the notion that whiteness is itself a form of property, Moreton-Robinson reflects that whiteness not only accumulates capital, but also '*social appreciation* as white people are recognised within the law primarily as property-owning subjects'.[48]

This accumulation of power and social appreciation makes the workings and effects of whiteness far-reaching and normalised to the point that it is comfortable and comforting to those it benefits. As Eve Tuck and Wayne Yang remind us, settler colonialism is an act of occupation, of making a home on stolen land in order to make whiteness comfortable – a property to be appreciated: 'Settlers come with the intention of making a new home on the land, a homemaking that insists on settler sovereignty over all things in their new domain.'[49] It is a specific intention of settler colonialism to 'domesticate' land and people, histories and knowledges – to make the settler colony 'homely' for those whom whiteness serves.[50] This is a domesticating impulse that has been described by Ghassan Hage as 'inhabiting the world by occupying it'.[51] Similarly, Shannon Sullivan has argued that whiteness is 'ontologically expansive'; it is a way of being in the world which presumes the right – and thus an implied innocence – 'to occupy any and all geographical, moral, psychological, linguistic, and other spaces'.[52] As Gomeroi writer Alison Whittaker recently expressed in her piece 'So White. So What': 'whiteness is a very wriggly structure with its innocence at its centre, and it will accommodate any incursions we throw'.[53]

Across contemporary institutions and interactions, we see ongoing efforts to make whiteness 'homely' through its expansion and accumulation. Helen Ngo argues in her work on racialised embodiments that whiteness allows some bodies, knowledges and feelings to be 'at home', while others are variously visitors, outsiders, outcasts or outlaws.[54]

Similarly, Sara Ahmed describes how whiteness enables some bodies to 'take up' space or to 'fit' institutions and structures precisely because these spaces and structures – as formations of unfinished histories of colonialism – *fit them.*[55] Spaces, including educational institutions such as schools and universities, expand to allow whiteness and those who benefit from it, while simultaneously making Others either hypervisible projects of inclusion or objects of exclusion.[56] These expansions normalise white sovereignty, ownership and domination in the settler colony, which make speakable questions like '*where are you really from?*', rendering non-white citizens perpetual visitors, migrants or outcasts of a white nation. The white possessive and its insistence on domestication is perhaps nowhere more apparent in public discourse than in the commonly heard declaration by white and non-white settlers alike that Indigenous people are 'ours': '*our Indigenous people*'.

The accumulation and expansion of whiteness not only occurs within interactions and institutions, but also through the production of social memories and amnesias of the racial state. The fantasies of white sovereignty, white superiority and the homeliness of settler colonialism are 'inscribed in textbooks, generated and regenerated in ceremonies and official holidays, concretized in statues, parks and monuments'.[57] Such active memorialising of the white nation thus takes material, epistemic and affective forms. Likewise, the collective amnesia of settler colonialism takes constant work; a constant teaching and learning of whiteness in order to disassociate and forget past and present violences of the settler state. Memory involves *labour*, writes Elizabeth Jelin: it is an activity 'that generates and transforms the social world'.[58] This is labour that can involve acting out the assumptive frameworks of whiteness, but it can also be labour that critically interprets the histories of state violence that continue to be viscerally felt and deeply experienced. As Sara Ahmed reflects, 'bodies remember such histories, even when we forget them'.[59] Dominance is never a finished project, and in the cracks of its supposedly smooth surface also lie counter-memory and resistance.

Because the homeliness of the settler state cracks under the truth of its violence and illegitimacy, the expansion of whiteness occurs through defensiveness and self-protection, expressed particularly through fears of 'Anglo decline' and the encroachment of 'other cultures'. This expansion produces and normalises systems of containment, carcerality and control. The bordering and policing practices of the settler colonial state visibly operate to defend white sovereignty, ownership and power. For instance, the disproportionate and violent incarceration of First Nations people, young and old, occurs through what Harry Blagg and Thalia Anthony describe as '*routinised* and *ubiquitous*' oppressive controls both inside and outside of prisons.[60] This is part of the 'detention industrial complex' that extends white control over Black and Brown lives, most explicitly through the mandatory detention of asylum seekers.[61] Similarly, the Islamophobic surveillance that expands into everyday life sanctions a racist discourse of fear in the settler colony and is emblematic of the attempt to project and secure the assumed innocence and homeliness of whiteness.[62] Such efforts to expand whiteness and the power of the racial state are also visible in the requirement for migrants to prove they have so-called 'Australian values' – a recent bordering technique in the settler colony's long history of migration and citizenship control.[63]

It is through enduring, occupying and expanding processes that whiteness can become both a pervasive *and* an elusive presence; what Kahnawà:ke Mohawk philosopher Taiaiake Alfred and Jeff Corntassel of the Cherokee Nation might call a shape-shifter.[64] Being a shape-shifter can make whiteness hard to grasp and hold down whilst simultaneously being easy to pass on or even pass off. This makes whiteness mutable over time, differently visible and differently felt depending on how one is positioned in systems of domination. Some people might not notice whiteness, while other people will be constantly aware of its presence and power in their lives. It can operate as a force so persuasive and so normalised that it can escape scrutiny by those of us enmeshed in its production.[65] This is how some Brown and Black people in Australia can benefit from, and work in the service of, settler colonial dispossessions of Indigenous people and the political power of whiteness, while at the same time experiencing racism, violence and exclusion due to white domination. Understanding whiteness as a structural formation and not merely reducible to 'skin colour' is also to understand that the settler colony's denial of Indigenous sovereignty under the white possessive shapes the lives of all Indigenous people, no matter what one 'looks like'.

While we each may have different relations to whiteness, it is clear that the settler colonial state has a vested interest in encouraging everyone – whether settlers, First Nations people, refugees, asylum seekers, or citizens within Britain and its other settler colonies – to learn and imbibe whiteness as superior, strong and dominant; the 'rightful' power of the colonised land. This does not mean that everyone who is taught whiteness through settler colonial institutions and public pedagogies experiences or takes up these lessons the same way. But it is the driving and active intention of learning whiteness in the settler colony that we are exploring: how the pedagogies of the state seek to secure white dominant futures.

Futurities of whiteness: the pedagogies of the settler colonial state

As we outlined in Chapter 1, education is not an innocent or apolitical activity. It is a practice and process that generates and contests social orders and interests. And yet, as Jessica Pykett has noted, debates about the changing relationship between the citizen and the state in a globalising world have tended to overlook education 'as a key site through which the state operates, through which citizen subjectivities are constituted and through which power is exercised'.[66] Indeed, while education has long been viewed as a 'soft power' in global geopolitics, it also – as Josh Frydenberg's words at the start of this book demonstrate – carries a militaristic force, symbolically and materially.[67] Frydenberg's suggestion that education is required to defend the nation goes to the heart of the relationship between education, whiteness and power. It indicates the unsettled nature of white sovereignty in Australia and the settler state's need to use institutions such as education to ensure that the lie of its legitimacy is accepted and reinforced. The setter colonial state requires whiteness to be learned so that, as Alison Whittaker has written, the colony can make and remake itself, keeping itself comfortable in its claim to sovereignty.[68]

'Pedagogies of the state' refer to the educational basis of this continual project of defending and relaying the racial state. The state itself is perpetually educative and its education institutions play a key role in processes of state-making. Pedagogies of the state are first and foremost about the relationship between the state and the people it governs. The work of this relationship is engaged with securing inheritances of power into the future. This is why the pedagogy of the state is a project of intergenerational relay; it brings certain histories into the present in order to secure particular futures. This pedagogical work can take multiple forms, as we have already touched upon: in the messages relayed through public holidays and memorialisation, in public images and narratives, and in commemorations of national 'leaders' and dates of the past. These enter into education curricula and systems – which are the main focus of this book – but they also operate beyond formal education in the material and cultural infrastructures of the nation: in monuments and sites, museums and archives, in social policy and institutions, and in anthems, food, arts and sport. It is pedagogic work that can be likened to what Zsuzsa Millei describes as the nationalism that is 'present in mundane and everyday practices'.[69]

This focus on pedagogy helps one to see how the structural formations of whiteness are *actively* transferred: people, ideas and institutions come together and interact to form particular educative relations. Importantly here, pedagogies of the state are not limited to state institutions. Certainly state policies and laws, and those who work in state institutions, are key to generating and enacting such pedagogies. However, state actors, private institutions, corporate enterprise and individuals all work in concert – whether they realise it or not – to produce the state and thus its attendant pedagogies. As we examine in the following chapters, corporate and media actors – while not usually identified as 'actors of the state' – often influence and sponsor material and cultural infrastructures for learning whiteness, producing pedagogies that are *of* the state in the sense that they seek to maintain its capitalist and settler colonial structures.

Our analysis of the epistemic, material and affective dimensions of learning whiteness in this book points towards the range of pedagogic modes through which the settler state produces relations of knowing, being and feeling. Learning whiteness through such pedagogies can appear innocent or natural; however, ultimately such lessons are deeply dehumanising, bolstering ongoing forms of state violence. Such pedagogies are a means for controlling and containing people, ideas, knowledge, cultures, feelings and communities in order to 'protect' whiteness. They create, for example, curriculum omissions, employment barriers and public backlash over different versions of the national story which cannot be separated from the state's more directly violent projects of racial control and containment: deaths in custody, dispossession, expulsion. Not only, then, is this pedagogy about securing inheritances and bringing certain parts of the past into the present, it is also about containing non-white knowledge and people in the past and building settler futurities – the imagination of settler colonialism as lasting into the future, unbroken and without alternatives.

There is, however, always a contest over how futures might be imagined and worked towards. Indeed, an important point is made by Julia Paulson and colleagues, who argue that schools and education institutions do not 'simply pass on messages agreed or struggled over elsewhere', but that education is itself a site where narratives – particularly understandings of 'difficult histories' and alternative futures – are actively constructed.[70] Bringing memory studies into conversation with education studies, their argument compels us to consider how whiteness is learned not through a process of unproblematised 'transmission', but through 'multiple, overlapping, conflicting and often unrelated understandings' of self, other and nation, which are actively created and contested in and through education.[71] How educational relations might be oriented towards justice – how education can challenge the futurities of the settler state and the learning of whiteness – is a question we return to in our concluding chapter. Indeed, the empowering thing about understanding whiteness as learned – as part of a pedagogy of the state – is that it makes it possible for such a pedagogy to be reconsidered and reshaped. It is not something that we are inescapably bound to; it can be collectively questioned and undone. But it is only through thoroughly knowing and understanding these lessons that we can reconsider them – and it is in Part II of this book that we examine these multidimensional lessons in detail.

PART II

LEARNING WHITENESS

3
Materialities

In order to understand how whiteness is cultivated through education, it is important to address how educational sites, institutions and systems are formed, literally speaking. This is to attend to the materialities of education: the economies of land, labour and matter which produce and sustain education. In the context of Australian settler colonialism, systems of education are linked to the foundational acts of seizing and occupying Indigenous land and waters, and dispossessing and exploiting Indigenous people. This is to say, every educational institution has been built with and through the material histories of settler colonialism and its corresponding project of capitalism. These histories are active and ongoing; the material production of education continues to be thoroughly implicated in the making and securing of whiteness today. In this chapter we examine the materialities of learning whiteness: education's land, bricks and mortar, and the divisions of labour and creations of value through which the white possessive is produced and sedimented.

Our discussions here also begin to map how these materialities are interconnected with the knowledges and feelings of learning whiteness, which are the focus of subsequent chapters in Part II. Understanding these dimensions as interlocking reveals how educational transformation requires, in the words of Sharon Stein, 'that we unlearn and disinvest from the inherited material, intellectual, and affective economies that frame our shared meanings and collective desires, and learn to invest in other forms of feeling, knowing, being, wanting, and relating'.[1] Indeed, our examination of how the settler colonial state teaches whiteness across material, epistemic and affective relations demonstrates how addressing racism in social and educational life cannot be achieved through piecemeal concessions, 'bracketed off' initiatives, or minor reforms. Rather, there must be a collective and systemic reckoning with unlearning and disinvesting from whiteness across all its operations.

We start by working with the concept of racial capitalism to explore how whiteness, settler colonialism and capitalism are intertwined.[2] As Onur Ulas Ince writes, capitalist relations have 'developed in and through colonial networks of commodities, peoples, ideas, and practices, which formed a planetary web of value chains'.[3] This is what Ince calls 'colonial capitalism' and we suggest that there is a need for greater recognition of how education has been enmeshed in its webs of valorisation and exploitation, both historically and today. For us, the concept of racial capitalism enables a focus on:

1) the practices of *enclosing/dispossessing* that stem from the capitalisation of Indigenous land, the containment of people and land, and the material construction of education systems and sites;
2) the practices of *dividing labour* that draw attention to how education rests upon racialised forms of classed work in institutions and systems – cleaning, building, administration, teaching, caring and so on;
3) the *extraction of value* through education, whether through material infrastructures and commodities, hierarchised people and knowledge, or the valorisation of educational assets, products and outputs.

By examining each of these relations of education and racial capitalism, we draw attention to how the material conditions and operations of education in the Australian settler colony make and remake systems of white domination. These materialities of education – how institutions are built, how labour is divided, how value is extracted – are the bricks and mortar of the state's pedagogies in whiteness. In short, through the concept of racial capitalism we show how education continues to build its house from race.[4]

Racial capitalism

The concept of racial capitalism has gained increasing traction as a means to address, in Satnam Virdee's words, 'capitalism's inherently racializing capacities'.[5] As Arun Kundnani explains, the term 'racial capitalism' was first used by anti-Apartheid activists in the 1970s to show

how South African racism was strengthened rather than weakened by capitalist growth, and the idea was expanded upon by Cedric Robinson, whose work we build on in this chapter.[6] However, recognising the co-articulation of racism and capitalism can be traced to a wider history of anti-colonial and anti-racist scholarship and struggle – even if these interventions did not draw explicitly on the term 'racial capitalism'. In Australia, a range of historical scholarship has highlighted the racialising character of capitalism, examining how hierarchic labour relations contoured the emerging colonial capitalist economy.[7] The past and present struggles of First Nations people to have their labour *and* their self-determination and sovereignty of land recognised demonstrates how the interlocking forces of colonialism and capitalism have been long and deeply understood. Prominent Indigenous campaigns, such as the Gurindji walk-off, show how the claim to land is concomitant with claims of workers' rights.[8]

Indeed, the concept of racial capitalism highlights how capital has always depended on the appropriation of land and the labour of enslaved, indentured and dispossessed people which, under transatlantic slavery and British colonialism, became bound to the colonial project of white supremacy. The racialised exploitation of land and labour under British settler colonialism enabled the creation of capital that encoded 'white ownership' into social, political and legal norms.[9] The development of colonialism through capitalism both required and produced hierarchised understandings of humanity (worker, capitalist and so on) through racialised processes of dehumanisation (dispossession, bondage, slavery). The construction of race, as Cedric Robinson's work has shown, has been central to capitalism's production of categorical social divisions that in turn support divisions in labour to create material value.[10] As Robinson outlines, 'The development, organization, and expansion of capitalist society pursued essentially racial directions ... As a material force, then, it could be expected that racialism would inevitably permeate the social structures emergent from capitalism.'[11]

Perhaps most fundamentally, racial capitalism draws attention to dehumanisation as a necessary condition of capitalist development. In Gargi Bhattacharyya's words, 'capitalism cannot function if we are all allowed to become fully human', because the accumulation of wealth for some requires the exploitation of life for others.[12] Capital, as Marx wrote, 'comes dripping from head to toe, from every pore, with blood and dirt'.[13] And, as Jodi Melamed explains, racism enshrines the hierarchic differentiation of people that capitalism *requires*:

> Capital can only be capital when it is accumulating, and it can only accumulate by producing and moving through relations of severe inequality among human groups – capitalists with the means of production/workers without the means of subsistence, creditors/debtors, conquerors of land made property/the dispossessed and removed. These antinomies of accumulation require loss, disposability, and the unequal differentiation of human value, and racism enshrines the inequalities that capitalism requires.[14]

Put in this way, racism is not outside of capitalism, but is its organising principle; it is the logic of capitalism's dehumanising premise – legitimising loss, disposability and the differentiation of human value. As Black Studies scholarship has long shown, the working of capitalism – from slavery and colonialism to their afterlives in the present – has required a systemic investment in and normalisation of Black suffering.[15] The history of racial capitalism is, as Sara Ahmed suggests, 'a history of those who are worn down, worn out; depletion *as* the extraction of surplus value or profit'.[16]

Of course, the history of racial capitalism is not fixed or unchanging. Social and political upheavals and challenges can create new conditions for racialisation and, with them, new capitalist orders. Jodi Melamed identifies how, after the Second World War, new projects of racial thinking emerged – including liberal multiculturalism and a self-declared anti-racism – which was able to update and accommodate the representations, codes and repertoires of white supremacy precisely by continuing to inscribe relative value to people within capitalist systems.[17] For example, within schools and universities, liberal multiculturalism became a means for 'diversity' and 'inclusion' to be valued and associated with feelings of 'doing good' insofar as these projects of racial thinking serviced rather than antagonised systems of racial oppression. More recently, we might understand global agendas for education under the United Nations Sustainable Development Goals as prioritising the incorporation and assimilation of children into systems of mass formal schooling without addressing, much less altering, the relationship between education, racism and the economy. Considerations of racism have been shown to be erased within education and international development policy and practice in favour of 'colour-blind' and technocratic approaches.[18] Therefore, global appeals to promote 'education for all' become a form of 'inclusion' designed to fit rather than challenge the needs of state–capital orders.

The maintenance of existing hierarchic systems can also be seen in discourses of 'learning loss' that have emerged after widespread school closures during the COVID-19 pandemic. Education policy and industry alike have been underlining the need for students to 'catch up' within systems of schooling rather than transforming the existing orders of those systems that are steeped in inequality. As Akil Bello reports, the concept of 'learning loss' in the USA emerged not from educational research, but from campaigns by publishers of tests and Wall Street consultants seeking to capitalise on concerns about 'widening racial disparities' in learning.[19] Policy preoccupations with 'learning loss' have gone hand in hand with the business of standardised testing, leading some educators to argue it entrenches deficit notions of Black, Hispanic and low-income children, stigmatising 'an entire generation as broken'.[20] As Bello concludes, 'perhaps the solution to educational problems created by socioeconomic conditions isn't paying test publishers more money to quantify and vilify students suffering from those very conditions'.[21] And yet, this is precisely how racial capitalism in education works.

Education as enclosure and dispossession

Enclosure and dispossession are foundational acts of capitalism and settler colonialism. Enclosure is the process of extracting value from land and, in doing so, dispossessing the people whose livelihoods and lifeworlds are connected to it. As Marx documented in the case of England, the emergence of capitalism was characterised by the mass enclosure of 'the commons' and subsequent dispossession of land through the displacement of peasants.[22] This act of enclosure and dispossession fundamentally altered the social relations of work and livelihood, but also the social relations of land.[23] In Marx's terms, this is a part of primitive accumulation; the act of enclosure was a moment when 'great masses' were 'forcibly torn from their subsistence, and hurled as free and "unattached" proletarians on the labour market. The expropriation of the agricultural producer, of the peasant, [their] separation from the soil, is the basis of the whole process.'[24] In other words, enclosure necessarily requires dispossessing, and this dispossessing involves radically denying the existence and worth of those dispossessed. For Marx, this dual process of enclosure and dispossession was central to the colonial relations that underpinned the development of capitalism, as it 'opened up fresh ground for the rising bourgeoisie'.[25]

Working with Aileen Moreton-Robinson's examination of the 'white possessive', enclosing/dispossessing can be understood as a fundamental act of settler colonial violence.[26] As Moreton-Robinson demonstrates, 'possessive logics' create the taken-for-granted conditions of settler colonialism in which land becomes propertied, a 'thing' to be claimed, occupied, laboured on and extracted from. In the Australian context, settler assertions of *terra nullius* – or 'nobody's land' – were used to wilfully dismiss the Indigenous knowledge, care and labour undertaken with the land, and rationalise the logics of the white possessive – claiming land as property to be 'settled' by colonialists for the accumulation of capital.[27] As historian Patrick Wolfe notes, 'settler colonialism introduced a zero-sum contest over land in which conflicting modes of production could not ultimately coexist'.[28] This foundational and ongoing logic of white possession reveals the mutuality of enclosure and dispossession; it seeks to render Indigenous people 'propertyless' and, therefore, as subjects of the colonial state to be controlled and contained. It lays bare the dehumanising premise of capitalism in which personhood is conceived in terms of property relations and labour value. And this is why capitalism is *constitutively* racial capitalism.

The declaration of *terra nullius* profoundly contours life in Australia today; it normalises settler 'ownership' of land and the very idea of Australia as a 'white' nation.[29] The logic of the white possessive continues to structure the settler colony's economy, in terms of relations of production and distribution, consumption and reproduction, and its organisation of economic interaction and exchange. For example, private property holds that land can be laboured on to extract wealth, making land something to be owned, developed and commodified. Racialised, classed and gendered patterns of land ownership, wealth accumulation and poverty, labour and debt that are in-built into the divisions of capitalism show how histories of enclosure/dispossession are not over, but actively configure 'colonial divisions of humanity' in the present.[30] This is to say, stolen land and white supremacy serve as conditions of possibility in the settler colonial capitalist economy today. This is what Byrd, Goldstein, Melamed and Reddy explore as 'economies of dispossession', arguing that dispossession 'not only presupposes and configures possession', but also works simultaneously to 'produce and delimit' what counts as personhood, property and value.[31]

Practices of enclosure/dispossession, therefore, are central to systems of education in settler colonies. For instance, as Sharon Stein documents in the US context, the Morrill Act of 1862 established public (state) land grants (or, perhaps more poignantly put, 'land grabs') that aided the building of higher education institutions.[32] Stein demonstrates how this expropriation of Indigenous land continues to re-articulate the practices of enclosure/dispossession by ignoring and thereby denying Indigenous claims to the land upon which these institutions sit. In Australia, the material development of educational institutions on stolen Indigenous lands also occurred through the state's taken-for-granted claim to the land. In other words, the 'white possessive' made the building of systems of colonial education possible.[33] And yet, the fact that settler appropriation of land and corresponding exclusions of Indigenous and non-white people have been the very basis of 'public' education systems in Australia is rarely acknowledged within historical analyses. For instance, the emergence of Australian higher education is often depicted in scholarship as a struggle over an education system that could serve 'the Australian community' as a 'common good', usually with a focus on class and gender.[34] Not only are Indigenous people and non-white communities largely absent from consideration, but what makes such constrained versions of 'the common', 'community' and 'public' possible within narratives of education is enclosure/dispossession – the dismissal of Indigenous sovereignty of public land, Indigenous knowledge and Indigenous people.

These material bases of settler colonialism are also the foundations for continued injustices in and through education. For example, in Australia the enclosure and dispossession of Indigenous land and people has extended to the epistemological objectification of Indigeneity itself. Institutions of education have been central to the enclosure and dispossession of Indigenous artefacts, materials and the remains of people, rendered 'objects' of scholarly interest and housed within universities and museums under the auspices of anthropological and scientific research.[35] Indeed, processes of enclosure/dispossession are continually recalibrated and reasserted. Take, for example, the case of an elite private school in Australia reported to have funded multi-million dollar upgrades to a council-owned public park in exchange for periods of exclusive access.[36] The logic of the white possessive works here in multiple ways; it not only legitimises claims to enclose and appropriate 'public' infrastructure for private gain but, in naming stolen land as 'public', it also obfuscates ongoing means of expropriation. Critiques of neoliberal privatisation that celebrate the 'publicness' of educational systems need to take better account of the violence of 'public' claims to knowledge, land and people, and how these 'public institutions' reinforce racial divisions even as they claim to broaden access to education.

The simultaneous enactment of appropriation and expropriation through education is perhaps nowhere more symbolically apparent than in the controversial case of flagpoles in schools. In 2004 the federal government under the conservative Liberal Party of John Howard introduced legislation to require all schools to fly the Australian flag in order to receive their allocation of federal government funding.[37] Entwined with the federal government's agenda to promote a nationalist curriculum framework for 'values education', schools were provided with AUS$1,500 to purchase or repair a flagpole.[38] Education here was unapologetically a site for the material and symbolic assertion of the white possessive. The planting of flagpoles stands as a claim to settler colonial ownership, which is of course premised on the appropriation of land. Schools were required to be the flag bearers of ongoing settler expropriation, their funding conditional upon this role. Up and down the country, material resources and labour were directed into this jingoistic project in the name of education. The funding of schools – providing resources for students and teachers – was staked to the logic of the white possessive. Here, enclosure/dispossession was not only foundational to the establishment of settler colonial schooling, but was being recalibrated and reasserted as an ongoing condition of it.

The divided labour of education

Racial capitalism works by creating and sustaining divisions in labour. Entwining gendered, classed, racialised and ableist systems of domination, divisions in labour emerge from, and themselves create, hierarchies of human life. Economies of dispossession under settler colonialism have been built on such divisions of humanity; colonisers were seen as 'civilised' whilst the colonised were rendered less-than-human and denied socio-legal personhood. By law and in practice people have been treated as part of the natural environment – or property – to be tamed, controlled and used, and whiteness was a core means by which these divisions became enshrined and normalised.[39] Such divisions in both labour and humanity continue today. Consider, for example, the precarious and underpaid labour of disproportionately Black and Brown cleaners, carers, transport and service staff who, throughout the COVID-19 pandemic, have been categorised as 'essential' to the economies of white settler colonies and the British metropole as well as 'disposable' within them.[40]

There is, of course, a well-established international literature that examines the ways in which education is intimately tied to creating and sustaining such divisions in labour. For instance, in Australia, *Making the Difference*, published in 1982, entered into a wave of sociological scholarship that sought to understand how schooling produced the inequalities of capitalist society rather than attenuating them.[41] Much of this literature focused on how education produces divisions in labour: 'sorting' students through grades, rankings and certifications; socialising students into relations of authority and control. However, here we train our attention on the divisions of labour required to *produce* education.

Take the ways in which white settlers amassed wealth in Australia to build 'public' institutions, often under the guise of benevolence. The wealth of both individual financiers as well as the settler colonial state was accumulated by enclosing/dispossessing stolen Indigenous land

and systemically exploiting labour on it. Indentured labour was prevalent in Australia, including the 'blackbirding' of tens of thousands of Pacific Islanders – forced or tricked to work on plantations from the 1860s until 1901.[42] From the late 1800s until the mid 1970s, thousands of Aboriginal girls were forced into domestic slavery in state institutions like the Cootamundra Domestic Training Home for Aboriginal Girls in New South Wales. Their humanity was denied and their labour exploited to service the violent operations of the settler colony – in the name of education and training.[43] Acts of labour exploitation, wage theft and indentured servitude were so systemic that it is impossible to separate the history of building infrastructures for education from the history of settler wealth extraction.[44]

Indeed, major settler reformers of the early colony were part of elite transnational networks of white men, whose supposedly 'progressive' views about expanding opportunities, rights and welfare were imbued with racism – specifically, with ideas of white superiority.[45] For example, Alfred Deakin, Australia's second prime minister, was instrumental in building public institutions and governance structures whilst also being one the chief architects of the White Australia policy – a policy designed explicitly to protect the white possessive.[46] Yet, the biographies of the 'great men' after which so many prominent educational institutions are named – Deakin, Macquarie, La Trobe – rarely connect their personal 'successes' with the practices of land dispossession and labour exploitation. We suggest that the failure to connect these acts is part of the violence of settler colonialism. Any account of the establishment of the 'great' public and education institutions of Australia must contend with the ways in which settler colonial status and wealth were accumulated through enclosure/dispossession and divided labour.

In the production of contemporary education, acts of divided labour are reiterated again and again, visible in different forms today. Lisa Hall's research in rural schools serving predominantly Aboriginal students highlights how the division between teaching and support work is classed, racialised and steeped in colonial relations.[47] Hall notes that Aboriginal teachers hold essential linguistic, cultural and historical knowledge but are often employed as lower paid teaching assistants or paraprofessionals and not considered core to the schools' function. Even for Aboriginal teachers who have received degrees from settler education institutions, both the process of qualification and the labour relationships following qualification continue to position them as a 'lower class' of worker.[48] This is despite the fact that non-Indigenous teachers in these schools rely heavily on Aboriginal teachers' linguistic and local knowledge. These racialised hierarchies of labour, and the overrepresentation of white teachers and leaders in schools and universities more broadly, shows how settler colonial education remains a site in which whiteness and capitalism are interlocked.[49]

Divisions in labour are also writ large in the ways knowledge is produced in contemporary higher education. Mayssoun Sukarieh and Stuart Tannock examine the racialised networks of subcontracted research production in universities in the global north, in which 'research assistants' located in the global south engage in the significant work of knowledge production – fieldwork, translation, local administration and so on – but whose labour is written out of research reporting and publications.[50] Indeed, under the paternalistic guise of 'capacity building', the work of northern experts in the global south is often positioned as a benevolent 'partnership'.[51] These kinds of divisions of labour reflect foundational colonial epistemological relations that structure the very formation of Western academic disciplines. As we elaborate in the next chapter, it is impossible to extricate the formation of the disciplines from the colonial relationships of 'knower' and 'known' and associated practices of knowledge extraction, exploitation and erasure. Thus, the global inequities in research knowledge production are an expression of these epistemological relations, delivered through the racialised divided labour of the academic workforce.

In addition to these divisions within the teaching, leadership and research workforces of education institutions there is a network of so-called 'non-core' labour. For example, maintenance, cleaning and grounds work has largely been outsourced, privatised and separated from the assumed 'core' of educational labour, teaching.[52] Such divisions reinforce bifurcated labour relations whereby rights and conditions of assumed 'core' staff are not extended to so-called 'non–core' staff members.[53] As with the example of Aboriginal teaching assistants/teachers in Hall's research, the core/non-core distinction does not reflect the highly interrelated labour required for education. This is to say, systems of education would simply not function without this full range of essential work. This was recognised by the US artist Mario Moore, whose powerful paintings and etchings highlight the divided and devalued labour within systems of education. Moore noted that the portraits of academics hung around Princeton University were notable for their lack of diversity, so he created portraits of the Black workers – cooks, groundskeepers and security guards – 'who really run things' and whose labour is required for teaching and learning to occur.[54] In Australia, the essential labour of cleaning and maintenance in schools and universities is often carried out by migrant workers, who have been shown to be vulnerable to exploitative conditions, including gross underpayment and systemic wage theft.[55] Racialised divisions in labour illuminate the racial dynamics of class divisions, bringing to the fore the central thesis of racial capitalism – the co-articulation of raced and classed structures.

Recognising the racialised divided labour of education draws attention to the full political economy of work which produces formal systems of education – from the labour of those who produce the materials required to build the infrastructures of education to the production of knowledge and the pedagogic practices of education. These are global networks of labour that create the material conditions for formal education: the production of pens and paper, computers, data platforms, bricks and mortar and steel; the differentiated labour within education institutions, such as the manual work of maintenance, the administrative work of operations and the academic work of teaching; and the daily and generational reproductive labour of care (including domestic cleaning, child care and the preparation of meals), essential to both education and society, but often made 'invisible' in analyses of market economies.[56] Racialised divisions in labour within, for and from education free up some as they capture others; this is how the white possessive is tied to the material economies of education.

Education as extracting value

Public systems of education are routinely defended for the value they bring to the nation-state – in terms of both economic and social returns – as well as the value they bring to individuals. Education, in this sense, creates material value. Consider, for instance, the value of educational credentials in the labour market, or the value of the kinds of knowledge individuals need in order to access and participate within educational and social systems. However, the valorisation of some forms of educational, social and economic life in capitalism necessarily involves the devaluing of others. As Lisa Marie Cacho writes, lives are 'legibly valuable' when they are assessed comparatively within prevailing economic, legal and political frameworks.[57] This means that those who are socially devalued do not get to decide the terms by which their lives are evaluated as meaningful or meaningless, as valuable or valueless. The settler colony casts out those deemed of little social value, their very existence being seen as a threat to the white possessive. This is how the systemic incarceration of Indigenous people or the expulsion and detention of refugees is 'rationalised' by the state.[58] Education, as we examine below, is bound up in making and sustaining these hierarchies of worth.

The lens of racial capitalism helps us to see how the production of value occurs *through* enclosing/dispossessing and dividing labour; it is only through these other practices that the value of people, land, knowledges, labour and materials is extracted and made. This brings us to consider how the creation and ascription of value in and through education can be understood as a fundamentally *extractive* process. Value is extracted across the commodification and capitalisation of education: through its buildings, data, curricula and so on.[59] For example, think of how universities market their cutting-edge or historically significant buildings and facilities; these assets continue to extract value for institutions – drawing student enrolment, research industry and business ventures alike. Universities in Australia are increasingly taking up the role of property developers and speculators, capitalising their stolen land to increase revenue streams. Western Sydney University has begun selling off its sprawling outer-metropolitan campuses to acquire and lease out high-rise urban buildings, a strategy of capitalisation characterised as 'future-proofing' the university's infrastructure.[60] Here its 'stake in the future' rearticulates the foundational acts of enclosure/dispossession through infrastructure valorisation; these are not simply acts of the past, but are reconfigured in the present to maintain the material futures of whiteness.[61]

We can also consider how educational data on, for example, students' academic performance are forms of capital linked to economies of dispossession. Such data are collected, published and used to accrue status and create educational competition between institutions. Behind 'valorised' school league-table results are stories of white opportunity hoarding and white flight. Christina Ho's analysis of school choice in Sydney found that public schools in poorer areas have been largely abandoned by 'Anglo Australians', and that within the city's wealthy suburbs there is a much higher proportion of migrant-background students in public schools than in private schools.[62] School choice and school markets operate through valorisation – the idea that some schools are more desirable than others – and this is enmeshed in racialised inclusions and exclusions.

The twinned forces of valuing and devaluing can also be seen in the commodification of school curricula. For example, schools can purchase a curriculum 'product' to make them more desirable in global education markets. Research on the Cambridge Assessment International Education syllabi has shown that the prestige of such products has been built on educational histories of asserting white superiority over colonised people and on the erasures of non-European knowledge.[63] In Australia, the Queensland government has produced an 'offshore program' involving the licensing of the Queensland curriculum for schools around the world. Its stated value is in the access it offers to 'English-speaking universities in Queensland, Australia and globally', with 'clients' across the United Arab Emirates, Papua New Guinea, China, Nauru and Taiwan.[64] These examples not only tell the story of the commodification of education, long familiar within critiques of neoliberalism; they also attest to the ways in which the hierarchies of value extracted through education are thoroughly and inextricably racialised.

Higher education in Australia has become a 'valuable' industry – contributing some 37.6 billion dollars to the national economy.[65] This value is not simply produced, it is extracted, most clearly from international students who pay significant tuition fees. Recent research on Chinese international students – who make up the largest proportion of international students in Australia – highlights how, despite their significant contribution to economic and social life in Australia, such students are afforded minimal protections in terms of their rights and well-being. This is in a context in which international students are faced with direct racism, social exclusion and systemic wage exploitation.[66] That international students' 'value' is exploited and extracted became starkly clear during the COVID-19 pandemic when, in the face of international travel restrictions and border closures, the Australian government denied welfare provision to those who were stuck in Australia. With job losses and housing insecurity, students increasingly turned to food banks, having been made to feel – as one student put it – like 'aliens that didn't belong here or inanimate objects or garbage'.[67] Education's extraction of value through racial capitalism's logic of dehumanisation echoes strongly here.

We can also look at the ways in which 'diversity' itself has become a valuable educational commodity. Markers of 'diversity' feed into institutional targets and metrics, rendering scholars and students of colour as indicators of calculable value. Appearing to foster a culture of 'diversity and inclusion' has become a pervasive, performative practice of liberal educational institutions. As Leigh Patel has so powerfully demonstrated, under settler colonialism the cultural, economic and social capital of educational institutions continue to be understood as 'white property'.[68] Patel explains how the valuing of 'diversity' in universities and colleges, even if performative, is met with a 'backlash' precisely because these institutions are governed by the proprietorial assumptions of whiteness. The extractive intentions of this valorisation of diversity are illuminated by the experiences of scholars of colour who are called upon to 'diversify' the curriculum and workforce, and perform a range of other cultural support services for the dominant white institution. This includes the 'invisible' and devalued labour of anti-racist care and service carried out by workers of colour.[69] Thunig and Jones draw on interviews with First Nations women academics in Australia to examine the experience of being expected to undertake invisible racialised work that is not recognised in the formal workload.[70] This work amounts to feeling like a 'black performer' and 'institutional cleaner', picking up the work that is deemed 'below' their non-Indigenous colleagues.

This extraction of value from academics who have historically been excluded from the academy enables the university to both project an image of diversity and avoid the material requirements of addressing its institutional whiteness. These forms of 'diversity' are valorised precisely because they do not disturb ongoing practices of enclosure/dispossession and the racialised divisions of labour. Moreover, there is a fundamental violence when Indigeneity becomes folded into 'diversity', as this diversity does nothing to recognise *or redress* the foundational acts of colonisation. These institutional projects are bound up in the systemic process of valorisation that both creates values *from* human life whilst at the same time devaluing it, a process constitutive of the relationship between education and racial capitalism. For, at the very same time that universities valorise what they can cannibalise – knowledge, cultural support, images of diversity – they diminish and reject efforts to unsettle liberal power hierarchies and disrupt the processes of racial capitalism.

The materialities of learning whiteness

In this chapter we have looked at the material conditions and material productions of education – particularly in its institutional form. The lens of racial capitalism draws attention to the enduring histories of dispossession and enclosure through which education systems in Australia were founded and which they continue to practise. This dispossession/enclosure is premised on the need to divide labour through dividing humanity, revealing how racialised exploitation is required for the functioning of education systems and institutions. Our analysis demonstrates how education can be examined for its extraction of value, how its logics of valorisation under capitalism and settler colonialism are premised on the exploitation and devaluing of life. Education is implicated in the creation of what Kundnani names as the boundaries between 'exploitable' and 'unexploitable', 'free' and 'unfree', 'deserving' and 'undeserving'.[71] Think of the unrelenting project of education to hold on to distinctions between 'success' and 'failure', 'literacy' and 'illiteracy', 'educated' and 'uneducated'. These are boundaries that are learned through the pedagogies of the state. And they are boundaries that racial capitalism requires in order to sustain ongoing, if reconfigured and upgraded, forms of enclosure/dispossession, divided labour and value extraction in the settler colony.

In highlighting these relations of racial capitalism as the 'materialities' of learning whiteness, we suggest that efforts to address educational inequalities in Australia must go far beyond questions of access and participation, inclusion and diversity. Relations of power are relayed not only through what Basil Bernstein influentially called the 'message systems' of schooling: curriculum, pedagogy and assessment.[72] The power and dominance of whiteness is also foundationally bolstered by the material economies of education – its land, labour and value. It is how the white possessive has structured education systems and practices. As Saidiya Hartman recently argued,

> The possessive investment in whiteness can't be rectified by learning 'how to be more antiracist.' It requires a radical divestment in the project of whiteness and a redistribution of wealth and resources. It requires abolition, the abolition of the carceral world, the abolition of capitalism. What is required is a remaking of the social order, and nothing short of that is going to make a difference.[73]

This points to the need to resist the impulse to 'resolve' the contradictions of valorisation that are produced by education systems. To draw on Lisa Marie Cacho's words, rather than attempt to resolve the contradictions of a system built on the degradation and refusal of humanity, there is a need to 'mobilize *against* preserving this way of life or the ways of knowing that this life preserves'.[74] This calls for new vocabularies and relational frameworks to imagine an education system in Australia that is divested from whiteness. And this is why we turn in the next chapters to the epistemic and affective economies of learning whiteness, examining how existing frameworks for knowing and feeling circulate through the educative projects of the settler colony, and considering how to imagine, learn and be otherwise.

4
Knowledges

Education can be understood most fundamentally as an epistemic project. It is, after all, a process through which knowledge is selected, relayed, created, revised, tested, ranked and so on. To be 'educated' is often associated with the acquisition of specialised knowledge, filtered through institutions such as schools and universities, and marked by credentials, certificates and degrees. The commonplace idea of education as the 'gaining' of knowledge has been central to its image as a driver of social progress, as an inherent force for good and as a tool for upliftment. Education is also seen as 'productive' in terms of its role in knowledge creation. Consider, for example, the research and teaching in universities that have been central to the making and expanding of knowledge across the sciences, arts, humanities and social sciences. However, this narrative of the productive good of education is much more complicated than it seems, not least when we consider how the institution of education has been central to sustaining the interests of the settler colonial state. As we discuss, the forms of knowledge and knowing that are advanced by educational institutions in Australia also service and sustain racial erasures, normative whiteness and the denial of ongoing settler colonial violence.

In this chapter we examine the *epistemic* production of whiteness in the Australian settler colony; how particular kinds of knowledges have been elevated and used within education, while other knowledges have been erased and distorted. This shows how education can be both a hopeful project and a violent one: knowledge and education can be generative, creative and freeing, but at the same time it can ruin, contain and control. Turning away from such tensions prevents all those involved in education from deeply contending with education's role in perpetuating racial injustices. Indeed, as we discuss through the work of Charles W. Mills, beliefs in settler colonial possession and superiority have been upheld within Australia's education system through its 'epistemologies of white ignorance'. As we reflect upon in the conclusion of this chapter, these epistemologies of ignorance need to be collectively reckoned with, in order to transgress and transform existing relations of thinking, knowing and learning.

Knowledge and coloniality

The project of settler colonialism has always also been an epistemic project. As Aileen Moreton-Robinson has discussed, the logic of white possession that structures the Australian settler colony manifests 'as part of common-sense knowledge, decision making, and socially-produced conventions and signs'.[1] In other words, the idea that settlers can make claims to ownership over everything, from land and resources to political and legal systems, is a purposefully constructed rationality, producing, mobilising and normalising specific epistemic frameworks in order to sustain itself. Epistemic erasure is part of the founding narrative of settler colonialism and it continues to this day. That Australia was 'discovered' by Europeans and settled by the British on the basis of *terra nullius* – nobody's land – erases the histories, knowledges and humanity of First Nations people. As recently as 2014, then prime minister Tony Abbott referred to Australia as 'nothing but bush' when colonial invasion first occurred, normalising contemporary claims to white possession.[2]

Such rationalisations of white ownership feed settler entitlement, structuring who is seen to be 'deserving' and 'undeserving' of resources, access and participation across all aspects of social life. Take, for example, the persistent dismissals of repeated requests by Anangu people for tourists to not ascend Uluru – a sacred site in Central Australia that has become a global icon for Australian tourism. After many years of campaigning, in 2019 Uluru was permanently closed to climbing. But in the weeks leading up to its closure, there was a surge of people undertaking the ascent, asserting settler entitlement and demonstrating an aggressive ignorance of Uluru's sacred significance. As Sammy Wilson, Chairman of the Uluru-Kata Tjuta National Park Board explained, 'Anangu have always held this place of Law. Other people have found it hard to understand what this means; they can't see it.'[3] What Wilson points to here is a sanctioned ignorance among settlers that permits the misunderstanding of life, land and law; the refusal to 'see' is used to maintain Australia *as* a white possession. The denial of Anangu laws is underpinned by epistemic rationalisations of settlement-as-entitlement, of the 'right' to white exploration and access and, perhaps most fundamentally, the refusal to recognise Indigenous knowledges, livelihoods, laws and existences.

These kinds of assumptive rationalities of white possession are, Moreton-Robinson argues, 'embedded everywhere in the landscape', not least through the regulatory mechanisms of the state that condition the possibility for Indigenous sovereignty.[4] 'It takes a great deal of work to maintain Canada, the United States, Hawai'i, New Zealand, and Australia as white possessions', writes Moreton-Robinson, '[t]he regulatory mechanisms of these nation-states are extremely busy reaffirming and reproducing this possessiveness through a process of perpetual Indigenous dispossession, ranging from the refusal of Indigenous sovereignty to overregulated piecemeal concessions.'[5] Here, Moreton-Robinson draws our attention to how the material processes of colonialism require the active destruction, misrepresentation and erasure of the knowledges, languages, histories and worldviews of the 'colonised'. As Frantz Fanon wrote in his treatise, *The Wretched of the Earth*, 'Colonialism is not satisfied merely with holding a people in its grip and emptying the brain of all form and content. By a kind of perverse logic, it turns to the past of oppressed people, and distorts, disfigures, and destroys it.'[6] In other words, colonial and racial domination is also about power and control over knowledge – over our understanding of ourselves and others, and over our pasts, presents and futures.

Reflecting on W.E.B. Du Bois' identification of the 'colour line' as the defining problem of the world under its history of white supremacy, Sabelo Ndvolu-Gatsheni observes that an 'epistemic line' cascades from the 'colour line', because the 'denial of humanity automatically disqualified one from epistemic virtue'.[7] In other words, racial and colonial domination refuses to recognise the oppressed *as* epistemic agents – as knowers and as knowledgeable. Consider the ways in which language and knowledge testing – from the dictation tests of the White Australia Policy in the first half of the twentieth century, to contemporary citizenship tests – have been used to systematically exclude linguistically and culturally diverse people from entering or staying in

Australia.[8] The tests only recognise knowledge in the narrow linguistic and cultural terms of the white settler state, rendering all those with rich epistemic resources that are outside of these terms 'undesirable' to the nation and, most fundamentally, disqualifying them from epistemic virtue – as knowledgeable and as knowers. As research on the experiences of African refugee background Australians shows, citizenship testing regimes have been 'driven by the desire to imprison refugees and other migrants into a narrow Anglo-Saxon worldview'.[9]

The ongoing project of settler colonialism, therefore, can also be understood as an act of what Boaventura de Sousa Santos calls 'epistemicide' – the destruction of knowledge.[10] Epistemicide has been foundational to settler colonialism's logic of elimination.[11] In Australia, the settler state and church missions forcibly took Indigenous children from their families and put them into settler institutions, with the explicit goal of 'assimilation': the simultaneous destruction of knowledges and relationships. Between one in three and one in ten Indigenous children were forcibly removed from their communities from 1910 to 1970. To be clear, this project of epistemicide had genocidal intent – its primary objective was to permanently remove the possibility for Indigenous people to perpetuate community.[12] This brings into sharp relief the reasons why ongoing anti-colonial and Indigenous sovereignty movements are also a struggle for what Ndvolu-Gatsheni calls *epistemic freedom*: 'the right to think, theorize, interpret the world, develop own methodologies and write from where one is located and unencumbered by Eurocentrism'.[13]

Education is not innocent in this epistemic destruction. As we explore below, educational institutions have been invested in particular knowledges and curricular prioritisations: what gets taught and how, what gets excluded and why. Looked at in this way, formalised education can be seen as a process of epistemic boundary maintenance. By setting boundaries around what counts as knowledge, and what counts as worth teaching, it is a form of radical exclusion: it evaporates what is outside its bounds; it is a form of 'abyssal thinking'.[14] The settler colonial state requires particular kinds of knowledge to be excluded and destroyed if the state is to be perceived as 'permanent' or 'legitimate'. As we discuss, education has been central to this 'settler futurity', which is why the epistemic lines produced by education do not simply need to be redrawn but require, rather, nothing short of an epistemological transformation.[15]

On the hope and violence of knowledge

The ever-present capacity of education to generate both hope and violence is what gives its epistemic project material force.[16] Consider the ways in which educational knowledge *has the capacity to build and also to ruin*. For example, specific areas of knowledge are selected into curricula, providing learners with the stepping stones to specialised expertise, credentials and careers. In this sense, curricular knowledge generates use and value for students and society; it becomes an asset that can be used to build opportunities as well as things – engineers and novelists alike craft worlds from such knowledge. But the codification and selection of knowledge within educational curricula can also erase and dispossess other forms of knowledge, experiences and histories, foreclosing and silencing other ways of thinking, being and relating to the world.

In his immensely generative book *Disciplining the Savages, Savaging the Disciplines*, Torres Strait Islander scholar Martin Nakata highlights the tensions of education's capacity to both build and ruin. Nakata considers how Indigenous people's 'hope for formal schooling' has been a 'political call to be rid of an intrusive form of governmentality set on entrenching Islander dependence on welfare'.[17] However, as Nakata examines, the 'inclusion' of Indigenous people within settler education systems was not accompanied by an inclusion of different knowledges and systems of learning. Nakata reflects on the experience of being a First Nations scholar in institutions grounded in Western disciplines and the continuous movement between different epistemological frames this involves: 'Negotiating between these is a transforming process of endless instances of learning and forgetting, of melding and keeping separate, of discarding and taking up, of continuity and discontinuity.'[18] The question for Nakata, then, is how to contend with and challenge the ways Western disciplinary traditions position Indigenous knowledge as something that is 'discursively bounded, ordered and organised by others and their sets of interests'.[19]

Indeed, these interests can be clearly seen in the ways educational curricula have actively displaced opportunities to address the very real ontological questions of Indigenous sovereignty and racial domination in Australia. Matilda Keynes and Beth Marsden have recently analysed school history syllabi and teaching materials at two historical moments of public reflection on state-sanctioned racism: the collective reckoning with discrimination after the Second World War and the 1997 release of the *Bringing them Home Report* on the forced removal of Aboriginal and Torres Strait Islander children.[20] Their analysis tracks how the curricular response at each moment obscured harms committed against Aboriginal people and closed down opportunities to explore questions of Indigenous sovereignty. Education systems might relay the knowledge to build bridges and roads or new scientific and technological infrastructures, but left to ruin are the kinds of knowledge that engage critically with the settler state and its ongoing structures of racial domination and coloniality. Indeed, as Keynes and Marsden demonstrate, Australian education works hard to legitimise and consolidate whiteness and its claims to settler colonial futurities.

The co-present hope and violence of education can also be identified in the ways educational knowledge *opens up possibilities at the same time as it holds things in place*. For example, knowledge can offer possibilities for the expansion of understanding – think about the new horizons of disciplinary and interdisciplinary knowledge created in universities and research industries, from new biosocial scientific approaches to emerging sociodigital research. New kinds of expert knowledge and biodata technologies are, among other things, being used to make genetic predictions about educational and life outcomes.[21] However, such expert knowledge can also operate as a 'carceral imagination', to draw on Ruha Benjamin's words. It can classify, control and corral people into delegated futures, futures structured by domination.[22] Indeed, research premised on the classification of people, either through explicit categories of 'race' or implicitly through categories such as 'culture', all too often turn away from analyses of *racism* – the very system that produces assumptive divisions of humanity.[23] In doing so, such research generates forms of knowledge that accepts and, thus, *holds in place* systems of racial domination.[24]

These carceral imaginaries saturate educational research and practice. Consider the use of educational metrics – from IQ testing and psychometrics historically steeped in the pseudosciences of eugenics and phrenology, to newer and ever more pervasive forms of assessing and ranking learners.[25] The pedagogical project of colonialism in Australia actively puts people and knowledge into hierarchies, not because these hierarchies are real, but because they provide an epistemological cover for the 'legitimacy' of the settler state.[26] Upholding the lie of white superiority has been an ongoing epistemic project of settler colonialism. As the work of Palawa scholar Maggie Walter suggests, there is a need to take seriously what Indigenous sovereignty means, not only in relation to the collection, use and ownership of data, but also in terms of the epistemological and political principles that underpin it.[27] The growing 'scientism' of educational research and practice continues to categorise students hierarchically, attaching notions of 'success' to some and 'failure' to others – filtering young people and holding them 'in their place'.

Indeed, whilst it would be convenient to think that racist hierarchies of educational 'capacity' or 'intelligence' live only in the past, they very much persist today, though often expressed through ideas of 'cultural' difference or disadvantage.[28] As Kamilaroi scholar Melitta Hogarth notes, the intensified focus on Indigenous educational disadvantage in contemporary education policy has perpetuated, rather than interrupted, deficit understandings of Indigenous children.[29] Her analysis reveals how Aboriginal and Torres Strait Islander people are presented as a homogeneous group in need of intervention, while the underlying structural racism of the Australian settler state – its policies of actively dispossessing Indigenous people of education – are left aside.[30] Education policy will not acknowledge whiteness as the problem, but instead pathologises all those who have the potential to disrupt it. This can also be seen time and again in social and education policy discourses concerning non-white migrant communities. Sandra Taylor and Ravinder Sidhu highlight, for instance, how refugee children in Australia have been positioned as 'medicalised subjects' by policies that are preoccupied with therapeutic interventions rather than recognising structural issues of inequality and exclusion.[31]

Our interest in the tensions of hope and violence in education also leads us to consider how *knowledge frees as well as domesticates*. Knowledge has the capacity for opening up potential and possibilities that can be a kind of freedom. For instance, universities are cast as places that, by definition, nurture such academic freedom. However, as a growing body of scholarship has shown, the modern history of disciplinary knowledge formation in universities is also the history of colonial appropriation, extraction and assimilation.[32] If universities are places where knowledge and minds are liberated, they are also places where knowledge and minds are colonised. Disciplines such as anthropology, archaeology, sociology and development studies have been formed through extractivist knowledge relations in which the specialised and honed knowledge systems of subaltern people are taken and domesticated, woven into the theories and canons of disciplinary specialisation, yet rendered invisible and inferior.[33] Such exploitation has formed the taken-for-granted Western *episteme* – or system of knowledge – that universities continue to be heavily invested in. The process of domestication leaves Other knowledges unrecognisable or 'undisciplined', deemed educationally worthless.

The disciplinary knowledge that is produced in universities directly shapes school curricula – the canons and texts taught in schools are usually drawn from the 'specialised' knowledge that is legitimised within the academy. This 'specialised' knowledge is argued to be a more powerful and important basis for education compared to the 'everyday knowledge' of students and communities.[34] Yet, the disciplinary knowledge produced in the academy is rarely acknowledged as often being, in fact, 'everyday knowledge' which has been extracted, appropriated and codified by research processes of academic knowledge production. Thus continue the assumptive hierarchies of knowledge: both schools and universities are implicated in teaching knowledge that is not *inherently* 'more important' or 'better', but is produced through uneven, exploitative and largely unaddressed relations of power. Indeed, drawing attention to this relationship between power and knowledge has been central to recent movements to decolonise the curriculum across the world, as part of global efforts to create new kinds of epistemic communities in an ongoing struggle with power/knowledge hierarchies.[35]

In Australia, young Indigenous people have been central in contesting these powerful regimes of knowledge. Consider *The Imagination Declaration*, produced in 2019 at the Garma Festival held on Yolngu Country in Arnhem Land, following the Uluru Statement from the Heart.[36] In this declaration, Indigenous knowledge, experience and culture is centred *as* the basis for knowledge creation: 'With 60,000 years of genius and imagination in our hearts and minds, we can be one of the groups of people that transform the future of life on earth, for the good of us all.'[37] Similarly, the Learn our Truth campaign, led by the National Indigenous Youth Education Coalition, is calling for schools to pledge to teach Aboriginal and Torres Strait Islander history, knowledges and experiences. The Coalition writes: 'The purpose of education since British colonisation for Aboriginal and Torres Strait Islander Peoples has been about assimilation where [Indigenous] histories, language and culture was deliberately suppressed and prohibited.' The Coalition identifies the need for 'direct and concerted action' in order to 'correct this course'.[38] They are asking educators to teach the truth of colonisation and support reflections on what continuing sovereignty means in school communities today.[39] This is part of a broader call by First Nations communities for truth telling across the country, a call that has recently been taken up by the Victorian state government's commitment to establish a truth-telling commission.[40]

The tensions of educational knowledge we are exploring here – its constitutive hope and violence – are what Indigenous and decolonial scholars have in various ways explored as the 'shine' and 'shadow' of colonial modernity. Walter Mignolo invokes coloniality and modernity as two sides of the same coin: coloniality is 'quite simply, the reverse and unavoidable side of "modernity" – its darker side, like the part of the moon we do not see when we observe it from the earth'.[41] Working with this idea, Cash Ahenakew and colleagues suggest that the 'shine' of modernity, its 'dialectical and universal reasoning, reflected in modern institutions and forms of organisation such as nation-states and democracy', cannot be disconnected from its 'shadow': 'expansionist control of lands, racism and epistemic violence'.[42] As the argument we build through this book demonstrates, the 'shine' of the modern institution of education – its hope as a social and individual 'good' – is inevitably accompanied by its 'shadow' – the violence of learning whiteness.

In the following section we train our attention on the shadow cast by what Charles Mills calls the 'epistemologies of white ignorance'.[43] The knowledge relayed and created through educational institutions is not only selective and partial, it is also active in making a cognitive system that perpetuates white supremacy. Understanding how education can uphold such epistemologies of white ignorance is crucial for confronting education's perpetuation of racial injustices. For it is precisely through an epistemology of ignorance that whiteness is learned.

Education and epistemologies of white ignorance

> *Imagine an ignorance that resists.*
> *Imagine an ignorance that fights back.*
> *Imagine an ignorance militant, aggressive, not to be intimidated, an ignorance that is active, dynamic, that refuses to go quietly – not at all confined to the illiterate and uneducated but propagated at the highest levels of the land, indeed presenting itself unblushingly as* knowledge.
>
> Charles W. Mills[44]

Political philosopher Charles W. Mills identifies ignorance as systemic – a kind of cognitive economy. Here, Mills contends with the ways in which whiteness is produced and defended through an active and dynamic – and at times aggressive – ignorance. In drawing and maintaining epistemic lines, education – commonly thought of as the acquisition of knowledge – is also implicated in the perpetuation of ignorance. In this sense, ignorance is not a passive 'absence' of knowledge. Nor is it an anomalous condition that is reducible to an individual's oversight or confined only to specific people. Ignorance is a system of thinking that is produced and required by political systems to secure, maintain and legitimise power.[45]

The systemic character of ignorance means it must be examined historically and structurally. European colonialism, settler colonialism and its attendant systems of white supremacy have been underpinned by a cognitive economy of what Mills calls 'white ignorance': 'the political economy of racial domination required a corresponding cognitive economy that would systematically darken the light of factual and normative inquiry'.[46] As art historian Bernard Smith famously described, a 'white blanket of forgetfulness' has been thrown over Australia's ongoing violence towards Indigenous people.[47] This is an ignorance that, in the words of Mills above, is 'propagated at the highest levels of the land'. It is indeed shamefully revealing that 'truth telling' – something that ought to be the basis of any social contract – has always been missing in Australian settler history and politics.[48] Indigenous-led movements for constitutional reform focus on the truth, squarely recognising and seeking to address the epistemic violence at the heart of settler colonialism – the ongoing erasures of Indigenous knowledge and voices in the histories and institutions of the nation.

The cognitive economy of white ignorance is, in Mills' words, active and dynamic: it is what establishes, maintains and normalises the lies of racial hierarchies and white superiority; it legitimises violence in the name of 'civilisation'; and it enables dehumanisation in pronouncements of liberty and equality. As Taylor and Habibis' recent research on Aboriginal people's perspectives on white ignorance highlights, such pervasive and systematic ignorance serves 'to create an impenetrable barrier of misrecognition', leading to 'stereotyping, judgementalism, disrespect and an assumed superiority'.[49] Here we see how the epistemology of white ignorance involves a deep cognitive naturalisation of whiteness designed to justify domination. Sabelo Ndvolu-Gatsheni demonstrates how academic research and public discourse are thoroughly implicated in the production of white ignorance, 'whitewashing' the atrocities of colonialism through claims of colonialism's 'benevolence', 'ethics' or economic 'benefits'.[50] The power of white ignorance is precisely that it presents itself as knowledge – as an indisputable, rational and even liberal orientation.[51] And, in the face of nominal juridical racial equality today, white ignorance, Mills suggests, tends to either deny the de facto perpetuation of white advantage or attribute it to 'differential white effort'.[52]

Indeed, one of the most insidious aspects of white ignorance is its capacity to normalise whiteness whilst condemning the violence of white supremacy. In other words, there is a failure to recognise liberal whiteness and white supremacy as being cut from the same cloth. As Mills argues, at the core of white ignorance today is the refusal to recognise the legacies of racist histories and their contemporary reformulations: 'the mystification of the past underwrites a mystification of the present'.[53] This mystification of the past is contained in the memories and amnesias of the state, made material through public and institutional pedagogies – for example, in school textbooks, official holidays, statues and monuments – as we discuss in the next chapter.[54] Zara Bain's analysis of the erasures of the atrocities of British colonialism in the UK education system illustrates this active forgetting and its purposeful production of selective historical memory.[55] This occurs in Australian education too. As just one example, when we (Arathi, Sophie and Jessica) were in primary school, we received a 'silver' coin in a small cardboard booklet as part of national celebrations of 200 years of British occupation. Given to every Australian child, the coin was to be prized and cherished, despite large Indigenous-led protests against the bicentenary.[56] That shiny coin asked us to collectively turn away from the shadows of Australia's past and present and, instead, to celebrate the project of settler colonialism and legitimise its future. Children were encouraged to draw a picture of themselves in the booklet on a space next to the coin, thus writing themselves into the white narrative of the nation.[57]

White ignorance, we suggest, functions in Australian education to erase, conditionally include and defend. *Erasure* can be seen in the omission of frontier violence in the teaching of Australian history in schools and in the obfuscation of experiences of migrant communities.[58] White ignorance can also be identified in processes of *conditional inclusion*; for example, the introduction of 'Asia Literacy' in 2010 in the then emerging national school curriculum. Knowledge of 'Asia' was understood as valuable only insofar as it could be exploited for the economic advancement of the Australian settler colony via the so-called 'Asian Century' rather than for its intrinsic epistemic worth.[59] And, perhaps most explicitly, an epistemology of white ignorance can be seen in the *active defence* of knowledge that perpetuates the lies of white superiority. For example, a 2014 review of the Australian Curriculum led by the conservative Liberal Party government concluded that 'history should be revised in order to properly recognise the impact and significance of Western civilisation and Australia's Judeo-Christian heritage, values and beliefs'.[60] This review was co-led by prominent conservative education advocate Kevin Donnelly, whose own publications are at pains to assert the 'good work' of Christianity and include catchphrases such as

'West is best'.[61] While the more recent 2021 review of the Australian Curriculum may represent a break from Donnelly's vision by including greater acknowledgement of the history of settler colonialism, it has attracted considerable conservative backlash.[62] The federal minister for education and youth, Alan Tudge, argued that it downplays 'Western civilisation' and presents an 'overly negative view of Australia' by teaching 'hatred' rather than 'love' of the nation.[63]

So active is this defence of the epistemic basis of whiteness that it draws heavy material investment. In 2018 over 3 billion dollars was bequeathed by the estate of the health-care businessman Paul Ramsey to establish a 'Centre for Western Civilisation' within the university sector. The Ramsey Centre did not proceed without controversy, but its aims stand as an example of the ways in which learning is 'weaponised' in Australia.[64] Rather than historicising understandings of Western civilisation – through the academic examination of Europe's entangled histories of capitalism and colonialism – proponents of the Centre underscore its purpose as celebrating the supposedly distinctive virtues of Western civilisation and shoring these up in public and academic life. Conservative Liberal Party politicians, including former prime ministers Tony Abbott and John Howard, were key drivers of the Centre's vision, invoking decades-long 'culture wars' about the threat to white Australia posed by 'leftist' academics and projects of multiculturalism. In Abbott's words, the Ramsey Centre was 'not merely *about* Western civilisation but *in favour* of it'.[65] Its goal of perpetuating epistemologies of white ignorance and, thus, maintaining white settler dominance could not be clearer: the Centre aims to 'foster a new generation of leaders with a deep knowledge and appreciation of Western civilisation and a desire to defend and promote it'.[66]

Such active distortions in education curricula not only provide the epistemic conditions for white ignorance to flourish but also enable it to be perpetuated as a form of white innocence. Not knowing, and turning away from the responsibility of knowing, is how whiteness can be invisible, unmarked, innocent – blissful in its ignorance – until, that is, it comes under threat. Then, white ignorance 'fights back' and 'refuses to go quietly', as Mills' words at the opening of this section suggest. This is what makes it an 'active' ignorance as well as an affective exchange (as we will examine more closely in the next chapter), rather than a mere 'absence' of knowledge. Recent attempts to address the epistemologies of white ignorance in the UK, for example, to promote anti-racist education and decolonise the curriculum, have been actively undermined and blocked by academics, politicians and public commentators. In 2020, members of the UK Conservative Party used a parliamentary debate to declare themselves unequivocally against critical race theory: 'we do not want teachers to teach their white pupils about white privilege and inherited racial guilt'.[67]

In Australia, the Institute of Public Affairs (IPA), a conservative think-tank with close ties to the Liberal Party, has attempted to lead political attacks against anti-racist education. For instance, Bella d'Abrera, the Director of the Foundations of Western Civilisation Program at the IPA, demanded that schools should retract the campaign 'Racism, No Way', arguing that 'Children need to be taught the basics of literacy and numeracy by their teachers, not turned into mini social justice activists who will grow up hating Australia because they believe it's racist.'[68] The IPA is particularly active in this defence of white ignorance, releasing a report in early 2021 which argues that 'the humanities are no longer concerned with the intellectual and cultural inheritance of Western Civilisation' and are instead preoccupied with identity politics, critical race theory and gender. Describing this as divisive, d'Abrera suggests that it is this education – rather than racism, sexism and ongoing material inequalities in Australia – that is 'preventing us from living together harmoniously as a cohesive society'.[69]

The settler colonial state continues to put up a range of defences to protect white ignorance. Take the ways in which state-led 'deradicalisation' programmes since 2015 have entered schools and community organisations in Australia, using racist tropes of the global 'war on terror' to normalise Islamophobia and create cultures of surveillance and fear.[70] Public schools – celebrated for their common good in the national imaginary – have become key sites for the racial state to enact and embed this politics of fear; the Muslim 'Other' is constructed as dangerous and trespassing socially, culturally and physically on Australian 'public' space.[71] In other words, education has become a mechanism through which the racial state is able to create conditional understandings of the 'public' itself; these operate as pedagogies through which one is to learn who can be at home in the settler colony, who must be domesticated and who must be expunged. And, in doing so, forms of state violence such as the mandatory detention of asylum seekers, Indigenous youth incarceration and other strategies of containment and repression are able to be enacted and justified in the so-called 'public best interest'. This is how epistemologies of white ignorance have violent, material, effects.

The materiality of this boundary-defining politics revealed itself clearly when the Australian federal government withdrew funding for selected Islamic private schools. As Emma Rowe has analysed, the review and subsequent funding freeze between 2015 and 2018 was an unprecedented government intervention into schooling that fed a wave of Islamophobic commentary in the Australian media and shored up notions of education as the property of whiteness.[72] Indeed, racist backlash to perceived threats to the whiteness of education systems is neither singular nor new in Australia. For example, the supposed 'over-representation' of Asian students in academically selective schools, particularly in institutions that have historically served white elites, has led to public expressions of white anxiety since the 1990s. Commentators in the media argued for the changing of selection processes, mourning a perceived loss of school cultures because of the wrong 'balance' or 'mix' of ethnic diversity.[73] Again, at the core of these discourses was the belief that these schools were the property and epistemological domain of whiteness. The fears expressed echoed racist notions of 'white replacement', albeit in their most genteel – and thus arguably publicly acceptable – guise. We see in these examples how white ignorance 'fights back' when it comes under threat, something we will explore further in the next chapter.

Transforming relations of knowledge and learning

As our discussions here have shown, there is a cognitive economy and an epistemic politics to whiteness. Whiteness is made and sustained through relations of knowledge and learning that are found across schools and universities, media and public discourse, laws and land. These relations of knowledge and learning are part of what we have been exploring in this book as the pedagogy of the settler colonial state. The pedagogy of the state is a force that is powerful and constantly being renewed. This renewal – the *work* of renewal – occurs through public, institutional, commercial and personal projects of white ignorance. It is an ignorance that acts like a shield to protect the legitimacy of the settler colonial state and insulate whiteness from the truth of its violence *and* the power of the Other.

It is important to emphasise that our examination of the educational production of white ignorance is not an exercise in epistemic relativism. While it is of course important to recognise the multiplicity and co-presence of knowledge-practices, what the analysis of ignorance helps to underline is how every knowledge-practice is inextricably tied to systems of power. This is not a relativist argument invoking banal pluralism or alternative facts about the history of settler colonialism; it is about training our attention on how whiteness, as a cognitive orientation enmeshed in the political system of settler colonialism, has a long and well-evidenced history of 'an aprioristic inclination to get certain kinds of things wrong'.[74] Truth and truth telling, as First Nations people have long argued, must be the basis of understanding past, present and future. Indeed, truthful knowledge relations cannot be separated from material forms of justice. As we discussed in the previous chapter, the white pedagogy of the state is felt and lived through material means, and these offer foundations through which epistemologies of white ignorance are cultivated. The project for racial justice must, then, involve redress for the harms created by material dispossession and extraction *through* projects of truth telling and epistemic justice.

Epistemologies of white ignorance ask citizens to be compliant and complicit with the white supremacist project of the settler colonial state. Those who choose not to take the lessons of the state 'correctly', to question white superiority, to seek truth telling, to resist the lessons of dominance, are typically cast as deviant. That is, the pedagogy of the state turns resistance to its lessons into deviance, thus marginalising those who propose different futures or seek justice for the destruction or distortion of knowledges. This marginalisation helps to bolster white dominance and is part of what makes white ignorance active. Therefore, challenging white ignorance requires fostering concepts and dialogues for building what Alison Holland articulates as 'a new relationship that recognises Indigenous sovereignty as the basis of redefining – and retelling the stories of – the nation'.[75] This is not just about acquiring new knowledge, but also about establishing radically different relations of learning. As a collective of Indigenous and settler scholars called the International Resilience Network points out, such relations should be guided by humility and a stance against oppression; cognisant of power and the interconnectedness of knowledge.[76]

To confront the epistemologies of white ignorance pursued by the settler colonial state, and to work for epistemic and material justice, takes courage, perseverance and solidarity, especially in the face of being made deviant. It also elicits a range of feelings. In the next chapter we examine how the settler colonial state oscillates between different feeling-states in order to protect whiteness and, in doing so, appeals to its citizens to ingest such affective lessons.

5
Feelings

Feelings move through the work of the state, creating connections and disconnections between people, ideas, histories, symbols, futures and things.[1] Feelings are not only mobile, they are 'mobilized and mobilizing' – moving people to act, respond, speak and believe.[2] As Sara Ahmed reflects, they 'align individuals with and against others, a process of alignment that shapes the very surface of collectives'.[3] And this is why feelings go beyond the individual; they carry and create complex politics that also operate 'in a realm beyond the personal and interpersonal'.[4] Feelings help make, relay and contest norms, practices and cultures of institutions at all levels, from families and schools to media and politics. Megan Boler suggests that the power of feelings can be the basis of collective and individual social resistance to injustices *as well as* a mode for social control: 'how we learn to internalize and enact roles and rules assigned to us within the dominant culture'.[5] Seen in this way, the political norms and public cultures of the settler colonial state are produced not only through material conditions and struggles over knowledge and meaning, but also through entwined and complex affective attachments.

As we have been discussing, the Australian settler colony is built upon the lie of legitimacy; the knowledge of unceded First Nations land and its unbroken civilisation is always looming, and yet it is constantly obscured, diminished and denied. Maintaining feelings towards a state that is longing for legitimacy in the face of perpetual uncertainty is an ongoing educative project. It calls upon a pedagogy of the state that has denial at its heart.[6] This involves not only denials of history – as we explored in the previous chapter with respect to the cultivation of white ignorance – but also the kinds of denial that can create and bolster deeply felt myths of, and beliefs in, white superiority. These are affective pedagogies which actively project pride, superiority and benevolence, while also putting up defences that emerge from fragility, woundedness, fear and anxiety.

Constructing an analysis of such affective pedagogies is difficult because feelings operate in powerful but sometimes elusive ways in social and educational spaces. They are influenced by personal and collective histories, memories, contexts, experiences and interactions. They also have no temporal bounds: feelings are layered and shifting, echoing and resurfacing across time. This is why our analysis of the role of feelings in the pedagogies of the state cannot follow a linear history: fear, pride, fragility or happiness neither unfold neatly nor are they simply resolved within the national story. Rather, these feelings are ever possible pasts-in-the-present, refracting, repeating and disturbing productions of whiteness. It is perhaps useful, then, to think about the temporalities of feelings in the settler state as elastic and recurring, haunted by violent pasts that are still present, and induced by a present that is tied up with amnesias, excisions and forgettings, always connecting the personal with the collective.[7] These complex, ongoing relations are what we term 'feeling-states'. By bringing together 'feeling' and 'states', we are indicating both the affective lessons encouraged through the educational work of the state *and* a state of being with particular feelings.

In the discussions that follow, we explore how affective lessons are passed between 'public' spheres and education institutions, in order to examine the oscillation between the feelings-states of happy benevolence and wounded fragility. The sections titled 'The happy benevolent state' and 'The wounded fragile state' move across time periods in a non-linear way and shift from public to institutional examples, indicating both the connections and reactions that are wrought by feelings in the settler state. While these two sections are separated for the purposes of our analysis, the feeling-states of happy benevolence and wounded fragility are interconnected. The multiple oscillations that occur when feelings are involved – between feeling-states, between the individual and the institutional, between the present and the past – are part of the pedagogy of the state that seeks to make whiteness homely and familiar. These oscillations serve to protect whiteness structurally, recentring desires for white dominance, possession and superiority, making these desires comfortable despite their injustices.

We begin by examining how affective lessons are deployed in the settler state through an intricate web of relations between publics, institutions, individuals and collectives. Importantly, these discussions show how such relations of whiteness can be learned through 'good feelings' – happiness and good intention – and this is precisely how the violence of settler colonialism is made acceptable in everyday life. Whiteness is not only learned by white supremacists, but also by 'good' people all over. And this is why it requires collective recognition and response.

Affective lessons

In order to understand both the movement of feelings and the way they attach to people, ideas, symbols, things and events, we take as our starting point the proposition put forward by Aileen Moreton-Robinson that the relationship between British settler colonialism and Australian national identity is constantly reiterated through 'a discourse of loss and recuperation'.[8] Moreton-Robinson explores how, in the 1990s and early 2000s, both the threat of Indigenous Native Title and increasing Asian immigration to Australia engendered ideas of loss in the settler imagination and acted 'to recenter white possession of the nation'.[9] This has been a recurring theme in the history of the settler colony. For example, historian Peter Cochrane examines how white Australians felt increasingly vulnerable from the 1870s onwards about 'threats from abroad' – namely, increased Chinese migration and the military rise of Japan. By the time of the First World War, white Australian leaders came to understand and rationalise Australia's military involvement not in terms of defeating enemies in Europe, but in terms of recuperating the colony's 'racial purity' in the face of perceived threats from Asia. In 1916, prime minister Billy Hughes told Australian men, 'I bid you go and fight for White Australia in France.'[10] More recently, fears of the perceived 'influx' of refugees and the supposed 'rise' of Islam echo this anxious preoccupation with the loss of white possession, dominance and 'purity', and the deeply felt need for their protection and recuperation.

Fear, uncertainty and anxiety connected to the loss of whiteness are familiar across settler colonies, embodied in what Eva Mackey calls 'settled expectations'.[11] This refers to the 'emotional, cultural and financial' attachments that settlers have to a way of life based on white property ownership and entitlement.[12] Her analysis identifies how local conflicts over land rights in Canada and the USA are sites of settler uncertainty and anger, expressed through actions, symbols and vocabularies in which 'settled expectations' are defended. The defence of settled expectations, Mackey argues, works to close down possibilities for reimagining existing relationships between land, belonging and sovereignty in settler colonies.[13] Similarly, Lisa Slater examines multiple sites of cultural production in Australia – memoirs, film, cultural tourism and policy – to show how so-called 'good white people' can express 'concern' and 'worry' for Indigenous people, while their steadfast evasion of Indigenous political will reveals an anxious desire for settler legitimacy and dominance.[14] In the analyses of Moreton-Robinson, Mackey and Slater, affective relations are shown to shape public discourse and legal and political structures as much as interpersonal and personal felt experience.

The desire for 'settled expectations' has meant settler colonial Australia has been continually invested in an image of itself as both at home and homely. That is, the state projects itself as 'at home' on the land, and the state is a homely place to be. Helen Ngo, in her book *The Habits of Racism*, examines three conceptions of the home: as a starting place, as a place to dwell and as a resting place.[15] The home as a starting place references a grounding in place and a place of embodied habit. Homeliness in the settler colony, then, requires a referencing of the white origins of the settler state, creating embodied everyday habits of whiteness. The home as a place to dwell invokes a settled place, a place to stay. In the context of settler colonialism, dwelling is vital to creating a home, and the comfort of whiteness is central to this.[16] And home as a resting place indicates that the home should be safe, secure and somewhere one does not have to defend or protect oneself. When the settler colonial state is threatened by disruptions to its attempts to make a home on stolen land, its resting place is disturbed and, we argue, it invokes defensive reactions towards those it sees as making the disturbances. For Ngo, the home becomes homely through habit; we become habituated to our surroundings such that we do not notice them so much – they are familiar, we are at ease.[17]

Homely spaces, where people may become habituated, invoke particular feelings. We are interested here in the different but connected layers of affect that make and disturb the homeliness of the settler colony, and how the production of feelings is part of a project of learning whiteness that has different effects on different people. For whiteness to be maintained in the settler colony, a sense of the continuity of its dominance needs to be felt. However, as we will show below, the crises and ruptures to this continuity of dominance also produce affective relations which can work to 'recentre' white possession. So, while dominance is never all encompassing, the resistances and questioning of white superiority often also spark the production of a pedagogy that seeks to secure whiteness. These too become affective lessons of the state. Take, for example, how efforts to debate and nuance the dominant story of the Australian nation have been met with aggression and backlash, operating, we argue, to 'school' the public in whiteness. This is seen repeatedly in Australia in struggles over the symbolic significance and meaning of ANZAC day. ANZAC day commemorates the military service of the Australian and New Zealand Army Corps in the First World War, and has come to include returned service people from other major offshore wars. But, as historians Marilyn Lake and Henry Reynolds have discussed, the promotion of ANZAC day by successive governments has functioned to entrench an Australian national identity based on the misrepresentation of history, promoting an 'imperialist, masculine, militarist event' that selectively narrates the nation.[18]

ANZAC celebrations have also become big business. Lucrative merchandising and advertising ventures have capitalised on and continue to mobilise affective attachments to the symbols and slogans of ANZAC, with some suggesting it is 'the most potent and popular brand going around in Australia'.[19] Such pedagogic enterprises have directly reached schools; the Department of Veteran Affairs has provided all schools in Australia with extensive and costly curriculum materials that centre the 'ANZAC spirit' and militarise the teaching of history.[20] In the early 2000s the federal government also invested in a programme to instil pride in school children for so-called Australian values. This included widely distributing to schools posters containing the Australian flag – a symbol of settler colonial rule – and a picture of a well-known First World War 'war hero' – a white man, apparently defending the settler colonial nation. The power of ANZAC mythology in Australia has 'come to serve as White Australia's creation myth'.[21] So defensive is the settler state in its assertion of this myth – across government, schools, private enterprise and media coverage – that 'to write about what's wrong with Anzac today is to court the charge of treason'.[22]

Indeed, this is what happened to Sudanese-Australian Yassmin Abdel-Magied, an ABC journalist and engineer who, on ANZAC day in 2017, posted to Facebook the message: 'Lest. We. Forget. (Manus, Nauru, Syria, Palestine...)'. Her post conveyed the need for a more complex and full national remembering, referring to sites of Australian human rights abuses – the mandatory detention centres for refugees at Manus and Nauru – as well as ongoing military conflicts and settler colonial violence felt across the world.[23] Reactions to Abdel-Magied's comments by politicians, journalists and members of the general public on social media were fiercely defensive.[24] Her post was labelled 'disrespectful', she was called 'a disgrace', and critics called on the ABC to sack her, suggesting the national public broadcaster 'should put Australia first'.[25] Abdel-Magied suffered death threats and was sent violent videos as a result of her post. Radio commentator Prue MacSween publicly declared that, if Abdel-Magied (who was now moving to London) had been going to stay in Australia, she would 'have been tempted to run her over'.[26]

The intense violence directed at Abdel-Magied was rationalised by the depth of feeling towards what ANZAC day symbolised – the benevolent and heroic whiteness of the settler state – and sought to shut out histories and presents that could tell a different story of it, a less homely and comforting one. The appeal to 'put Australia first' portrays an Australia that is wholly good, altruistic, strong and brave. This leaves no room for recognising the violence of the settler state, including Indigenous dispossession and the incarceration of First Nations people and asylum seekers in onshore and offshore detention camps. It also forecloses more complex debate about the consequences of war and invasion that Abdel-Magied (and others) were pointing to, as this kind of conversation gets silenced by the defensiveness expressed on behalf of the settler state. While there has been much commentary on how this incident highlighted the prevalence of racism and hate speech in Australia, it also represented a public moment when the questioning of white dominance in the settler colony created an emotionally charged defensive reaction.[27] The scale of the rage unleashed upon Abdel-Magied, even after she had removed her post, illustrates how the pedagogy of the state – those attempts by media, politicians and the public to delimit what is thinkable and speakable – can be defensive but also act with violent authority.

This example powerfully illustrates what we call 'feeling-states'. The structures of the settler colonial 'state' and the personal 'state' of being with 'feeling' came together in the backlash against Abdel-Magied. The racism directed towards her – as a Black, Muslim Australian – was expressed through feelings of being wounded or threatened. She apparently hurt the settler colonial state as well as those individuals who feel invested in the 'comforting' whiteness of the state. That such racism and the wounds to whiteness that underpinned it were possible in public discourse points to how powerful the attachments to white superiority and white possession are in the settler colony. Feelings are social, political, cultural and psychological, embodied and exchanged.

The response to Abdel-Magied, as well as the promotion of ANZAC chauvinism by governments and industry alike, show how pedagogies of the state aggressively invest in particular feelings (and disregard others, such as those associated with the effects of racism that Abdel-Magied experienced); namely, feelings that justify past and present white dominance and its security and certainty in the future. Implied here is the comforting promise that such feeling-states 'are justly earned by those who enjoy them'.[28] As Sharon Stein writes, 'when the fulfilment of these promises is threatened, whether because someone challenges their legitimacy or because the systems that once guaranteed them are failing on their own accord, people often become overwhelmed and defensive'.[29] As we show in the next sections, it is through such complex feeling-states that whiteness can be asserted, struggled over, resisted, defended and learned.

The happy benevolent state

Contemporary Australia works hard to produce an image of itself as a happy, inclusive, fun-loving and friendly society; a so-called 'lucky country' of 'mateship' and 'fair go' where all can feel at home.[30] A self-conscious projection, this image is central to the settler story of good intentions and benevolence. Yet, whiteness and the ongoing violence of settler colonialism looms large in this picture of happy benevolence. This is perhaps most clearly seen in the establishment of the system of 'Aboriginal Protectorates' which operated in the nineteenth and twentieth centuries across Australia. In the name of care, benevolence and 'protection', the system was used to violently control, assimilate, surveil and dehumanise Aboriginal people.[31] Aboriginal people were subjected to dispossession which moved them off their lands and onto missions and reserves, controlled their movements through exemption certificates known as 'dog tags', and regulated their employment, finances and family life.[32] Narratives of white care and concern fed into government directives to remove Aboriginal and Torres Strait Islander children from their families throughout this period, producing what is now known as the Stolen Generations.[33]

Underpinning the benevolence of the settler state was an assertion that white families and institutions such as schools were more suitable for caring for and educating Indigenous children. This positioned whiteness as well-meaning, superior (in intellect, culture and civilisation) and capable of providing a good home. As Jane Carey explores, in the first half of the twentieth century white women assumed a public role within organisations such as the National Council of Women and the Free Kindergarten Union in Victoria, to lead extensive educational and social campaigns among white settlers. However, at the centre of such outreach was an enthusiastic promotion of eugenics and the desire for 'white racial betterment' to counter settler anxieties of 'racial degeneracy'.[34] Such affective attachments to white domination continue today, with more Aboriginal children being removed from their families in recent years than during the period of the Stolen Generations,[35] and the image of the strong, white, caring family continuing to animate media reports and commentary.[36]

There are many ways in which such attachments to whiteness are learned over time and across different kinds of pedagogies. Our earlier discussion of the ANZAC day celebrations offered an insight into such pedagogic investments. Cultural productions of whiteness such as this abound in the 'everyday life' of the settler colony – through commemorations and public holidays, within museums and schools, in songs and art, through corporate advertising and government campaigns, and within interpersonal encounters and exchanges. A visually striking example to consider here is the branding, symbols and iconography attached to Australia Day, the national holiday which celebrates the 'arrival' of settlers instead of recognising it as violent invasion. Aboriginal and Torres Strait Islander activists have long interrogated this state-led celebration of violence, for example through the Day of Mourning and Protest in 1938, and ongoing movements to recognise Australia Day as 'invasion day'.[37] In 2010, the National Australia Day Council (a not-for-profit government-owned company) launched an advertising campaign with a series of vivid posters designed to celebrate the supposed 'good things' about living in Australia and 'being Australian'.[38] Picking up the military theme so important to ANZAC day, they were also designed to stylistically reference Second World War propaganda-style posters.[39]

The posters featured images of predominantly white-looking people standing in powerful and assertive positions alongside militaristic iconography; they are muscular, determined and confident in adopting their salute-like poses. Clearly the branding was an attempt at playfulness, referencing the happy Aussie of the 'fair go': the images centre on the 'Aussie barbeque', with the central characters clutching sausages, chops and a frisbee; the formation of flying jets in the sky are actually tongs; while 'Man your eskys' (portable coolers) and 'BBQ like you've never BBQ'd before' rhetorically announce the Australia Day 'call to arms'. This apparent playfulness feeds a representation of the settler state as happy and proud. The militaristic iconography, however, glosses over the military force of the settler state: the forces that led the Frontier Wars; the forces that continue to uphold border control involving the forced detention of refugees; and the forces of the police and welfare practices that are shown again and again to be structured by racism.[40] These posters, then, can be seen as an attempt to secure the legitimacy of the happy and proud settler state, a place of homeliness and security within which colonial sovereignty – and the whiteness that underpins it – is publicly asserted and urged to be collectively felt.

Indeed, the posters' slogan, 'however you celebrate, do yourself proud', gestures towards a nation that is accepting of diversity so long as this does not threaten white possession. This message plays out frequently, not only in how diversity is 'managed' within national migration policies, but also in institutions and between individuals. *Be grateful we let you in, don't rock the boat.* Here, not only is settler violence denied and white ownership assumed, but there is also an affective impulse towards what Sara Ahmed calls 'happy multiculturalism'.[41] Happy multiculturalism 'welcomes' diversity in schools, universities, workplaces, etc., and in doing so whiteness is seen as good and helpful, a homely, happy, kind and generous host. It is thus intimately connected to the feeling-states of white benevolence. However, this appeal to happiness does nothing to dislodge structures of racism within institutions. Nor does it attend to the interpersonal dynamics of what Helen Ngo calls the 'habits of racism' – those interactions, moments and habituated responses that repeatedly remind non-white Australians they can never truly feel 'at home'.[42] The lesson is that non-white people should feel grateful and proud to be 'let in' or 'accepted', such that whiteness can maintain its desires for dominance, benevolence and ownership. If anything, it is another technique to centre and secure whiteness – to allow whiteness to feel at home, and for it to 'domesticate' all those it conditionally includes.[43]

These affective pedagogies can be seen within the multicultural policy discourse that emerged from the early 1970s in light of protest and campaigning for greater recognition of migrant and Indigenous rights.[44] Government policies over the next two decades – including a number of significant school-based curriculum developments – characterised multiculturalism as a 'celebration' of diverse cultural traditions.[45] This policy shift was used to position the settler state as moving away from an overtly racist past; the feeling-state of happy inclusion associated with this reform was a way of differentiating present forms of 'doing good' from a past deemed 'bad'. However, as many critics have observed, it was also a way of concealing enduring inequalities and injustices.[46] Such assertions of the happy benevolent state continued after 1996 under the conservative leadership of John Howard, though official multiculturalism was replaced with ideas of Australian values and heritage in order to create, in Howard's terms, 'a projection and outpost, if you like, of the best of western civilisation in this part of the world'.[47] Such powerful lessons in white happiness continue today, allowing the pedagogies of the state to deny the causes and impacts of racism. As a vivid case in point, since 1999 Australia has celebrated what it calls 'Harmony Day' in place of recognising the United Nations International Day for the Elimination of Racial Discrimination.[48]

These cultural discourses are mirrored and enacted in schools. Our discussions in previous chapters about white opportunity hoarding and 'white flight' from ethnically diverse schools show how contemporary education markets in Australia are underpinned by a deeply felt belief that schools should serve the interests of whiteness. Consider also Emma Rowe's study of the parent lobby groups in Melbourne campaigning during the first decades of the twenty-first century for new schools in their neighbourhoods. She shows how whiteness 'played out within the local education market as an essential constituent for leveraging advantage and collectively evading differences'.[49] Indeed, we suggest that education operates as a comfort zone for whiteness. We are reminded here of a poignant cartoon by Matt Golding published in 2016 in the Melbourne-based newspaper *The Age*, alongside a story about white flight from Fitzroy primary school in inner Melbourne. The cartoon depicts a white child asking, 'Mum, why don't I go to the school across the road? It's in our zone!' As a Brown schoolchild walks past their front gate, the white mother replies: 'Yes ... but it's also out of our comfort zone.'[50] This cartoon speaks to the affective dimensions of white flight, the fear of losing the security and comfort of white dominance in the school and community. Such feeling-states bolster the epistemic and material inequalities that are sustained by white dominance.

Happy multiculturalism maintains comfort zones for whiteness and is a means for the settler state to project a present and future homeliness. Such white homeliness is articulated around a notion of cultural diversity and inclusion in which a benevolent hand is extended to diverse ethnic groups, but only insofar as they don't disturb the comfort and dominance of whiteness. In this way, a 'young' 'migrant' Australia is invited to reap the rewards of the settler state on stolen land. However, happy multiculturalism is conditional. Inclusion and diversity are acceptable only when they are understood not to threaten Australia's 'connection' to Empire (Britain) and its associated orders of whiteness. For example, questions of settler sovereignty, anxieties around migrant success and fears of white 'loss' all indicate the limit points of happy multiculturalism. When the images of strength, benevolence, goodness, care and dominance of the settler colonial state are perceived to be threatened, we see time and again outbursts of white defensiveness. At these moments the state is projected as fragile and wounded, and whiteness is positioned as being in need of protection and recuperation. Here, the interrelationship between the feeling-states of happy benevolence and wounded fragility become clear. And, as we turn to explore now, fragility and woundedness are used as recurring defences for whiteness, foreclosing possibilities for other ways of learning to be, think and feel in the settler colony.

The wounded fragile state

The happy benevolent state is produced through delusions of grandeur – its confident projection of white superiority and ownership is, in fact, deeply vulnerable, because it is a lie. This gives rise to another kind of projection – a wounded, fragile state in need of constant protection and defence. In this section we explore how feeling-states of paranoia, anxiety and fear bolster the idea that whiteness needs to be protected, working to rationalise violent racism in the forms of dehumanisation, expulsion and incarceration. The long-held, indeed, *founding* desire to protect whiteness in the settler colonial state has involved ongoing strategies to project the non-white Other as an inherent threat. These pedagogic messages are not only relayed through official state policies, but are also supported through public and educational cultures. Such cultural pedagogies work with and through exclusionary state policies to engender within the settler population feelings of fear of the racialised Other and to reinforce the power of whiteness.[51]

This can be seen, for example, in the outrage and anger in response to comments by Aboriginal activist Tarneen Onus-Williams at an Invasion Day protest in Melbourne in 2018. In contrast to the feeling-states of pride and playfulness displayed on the Australia Day posters discussed above, Onus-Williams' speech at the rally called for the abolition of Australia Day and questioned the very existence of Colony Australia: 'We have not organised this to change the date. We have organised this to abolish Australia Day because f*** Australia. F*** Australia, I hope it f***ing burns to the ground.'[52] The anger Onus-Williams expressed towards the long and devastating effects of colonialism and years of state policies that have undermined First Nations sovereignty and self-determination was met with white defensiveness and anger. Politicians and media were outraged at what they perceived as an incitement to violence against the Australian state, the threat of a First Nations backlash against the powerful and benevolent white nation being positioned as ungrateful and disrespectful. This scenario demonstrates both the fragility of the settler state and of the white dominance that underpins it, as well as the capacity to use this supposed fragility to avoid the real confrontation, which involves being truly accountable for a history of violence and the ongoing harms of state institutions.

Importantly, it is both the 'dangerous' Aboriginal activist (internal threat) and the 'menacing' racialised immigrant (external threat) that invoke these defensive responses. The constantly looming external threat has been explored by poet and writer Yu Ouyang in his detailed analysis of the obsession with racial purity and fear of Chinese 'invasion' within Australian settler literature. Ouyang examines what he calls a 'century of paranoia' – from 1888 to 1988 – in which 'celebrations' of white settlement in Australia within literary and media discourse depended on the maintenance of racial exclusion: 'For Australia to survive as a nation, Chinese must keep out.'[53] Ouyang shows how, in influential magazines such as *The Bulletin* as well as works of settler fiction, Chinese people have been persistently portrayed as sinful, diseased, dishonest and vengeful. In these paranoid depictions, whiteness, whilst celebrated, is projected as fragile and at risk. Chinese people are excluded and denigrated as cruel, callous and immoral, as a means of securing the continuation of settler domination. Ouyang's analysis demonstrates how media and cultural texts work in explicitly pedagogic ways, inciting and enabling racism in order to protect whiteness from perceived invasion and impurity. These affective pedagogies engender feeling-states of woundedness and fragility which reverberate into the present.

In recent decades, violent anti-Muslim racism has become common in Australia, spurred in part by the global Islamophobia of the post-2001 'war on terror'. However, this anti-Muslim racism is also connected to the longer history of what Anne Aly and David Walker call the 'survivalist anxiety' of a settler colonial state which has always grappled with the presence of Muslims.[54] They trace how, since the late 1970s, the Australian popular media has been preoccupied with the idea of an Islamic resurgence, and how the dominant representation of the Middle East was centred on the image of the 'Arab terrorist'. From the mid 1990s onwards, the media fuelled moral panics about 'crime gangs' of 'Middle Eastern youths' in Australia's cities, with racist commentators and politicians invoking Islam as inherently violent in contradistinction to the goodness of 'Australian culture'.[55] From around 2000, rising anti-immigrant and anti-refugee politics in Australia was bolstered though media representations that took up explicit Islamophobic positions. This was also seen in the reporting of the 2005 riot in the Sydney suburb of Cronulla which was provoked by claims to territory. A group of young, white male surf-lifesavers asserted that the Cronulla beach 'belonged' to them, affronted by the use of the beach by Muslim Lebanese-background men from the inland suburbs.[56] Indeed, the perceived threat to white possession and white superiority runs through this history of Islamophobia, conjuring an image of Australia as a peaceful, rightful and good white society, wounded by the presence of the Muslim Other.[57]

The threat of the racialised Other is invoked through dehumanising imagery across popular discourse. Ghassan Hage explores how animalistic tropes – such as monkeys, snakes, dogs or wolves – are frequently drawn on to portray racialised Others. Such dehumanising imagery is used to convey whiteness as superior, and as a rationale for whiteness to control and contain, tame and discipline.[58] The pedagogy of the state teaches that this is acceptable, enabling racist school-yard bullies and politicians alike. This public acceptance of dehumanisation, particularly against Indigenous people, was blatantly apparent in the racism directed at Australian Rules footballer Adam Goodes. Like other Aboriginal players before him, Goodes experienced both institutional racism and repeated racial abuse from the crowds watching him play. In one particularly cruel instance in 2013, a girl in the crowd called him an ape. Despite Goodes using his platform to engage patiently with the public about the need to recognise racism and its deeply felt impact, as well as the importance of education in addressing it, the abuse against him escalated and continued unabated for months. This was spurred by the tabloid press, which consistently portrayed him as a threat to the white nation for naming the racism he experienced, for his apparent curtailing of the crowd's 'right to have fun' and for his unapologetic Blackness.[59]

The threat of Blackness is starkly evident in how the justice system works as a site of continued state violence against First Nations people, including young people; extraordinary incarceration rates, as well as prison abuse and deaths in custody, are logics of the system rather than being aberrant to it.[60] Similarly, the wounded fragile state criminalises asylum seekers, incarcerating them in offshore detention camps through policies that claim to be about protection.[61] This criminalising of the Other runs through the education system too. Within schools, those who deviate from the dominant culture are disciplined and expunged and made subjects of reform; Indigenous students and some minoritised groups are more likely to be suspended, expelled or disciplined for 'poor behaviour'.[62] Since 2015, with the publication of *Preventing Violent Extremism and Radicalism in Australia* by the federal Attorney General Department, schools and teachers have been implicated in the surveillance of young people considered a possible threat.[63] In particular, young Muslim people have been the target of such educational surveillance and associated 'de-radicalisation' programmes, which not only pathologise them – itself a form of racism – but also entrench the existing structural racism they experience.[64] Those who cannot be assimilated to whiteness – who refuse to feel and act in the interests of whiteness – are surveilled, removed, disciplined, expunged or locked up.

Affective interactions, encounters, habits and orientations in schools and universities can allow whiteness to feel at home, secure, comfortable and so in-the-right-place that it remains unseen and unspoken by many – and determinedly protected by institutions when it is called out. For example, in Brisbane in 2019, a white nine-year-old primary school student who chose not to stand for the national anthem was given a lunchtime detention for disobedience.[65] She was told she could not continue to protest and had to either stand for the anthem or leave the assembly area. Her purpose in remaining seated was to demonstrate her opposition to singing that Australia is 'young and free' and to draw attention to institutionalised racism. The disciplinary response by the school demonstrates the institutional commitment to settler colonial feelings of legitimacy.

There remains a significant need for schools and other sites of learning to understand and address their affective attachments to whiteness. Research in Melbourne primary schools showed that white teachers felt 'uncomfortable' talking about cultural diversity, due to a lack of knowledge and experience. This meant they were teaching their lessons about Australian national identity as though it was 'commensurate to white racial and Anglo-Australian cultural identity'.[66] In this example, the comfort zones of whiteness – its familiarity and continuity – are protected through classroom pedagogies that render anything other than whiteness unspeakable. The care taken to not disturb the comfort of whiteness was recounted by African Australian students in recent research by Jonnell Uptin. One participant, Hannah, described how her teacher was 'scared that he's gonna say something to offend us'.[67] Recalling how the teacher spoke about Tichiba, a character from *The Crucible*, Hannah explained, 'He was *so* careful because she was Black.'[68] The African Australian students in Uptin's study noted their differential treatment by teachers and how the teachers' desire to not be racially offensive was 'another way of separating them instead of including them'.[69]

This uncertainty and fear on the part of teachers could be understood as a form of white evasion, something that Yukari Takimoto Amos, following Alice McIntyre, argues involves a 'culture of niceness', in which 'whites commit themselves to avoiding confrontation and keeping relationships pleasant at all costs'.[70] This pleasantness or niceness, which can be a mask for discomfort, is an expression of the feeling-state of happy benevolence, but is also a defence against the discomfort of threats to whiteness. Research in the United States has explored how white pre-service teachers employ a range of emotional 'defences' to avoid the discomfort of addressing hegemonic whiteness in discussions about racial justice in schools.[71] Bree Picower calls these 'tools of whiteness', which can include fear of the Other, anger at the displacement of whiteness, deflection of guilt and feeling overwhelmed.[72] While there is little research published on teachers' feelings in relation to racism in education in Australia, each of us have felt personally, and seen among our colleagues and students, 'push back', fear and anguish (often expressed in terms of a lack of confidence) in courses that address multiculturalism, Indigenous education and racism. These challenging feeling-states are brought about when the tensions between confirming and questioning the affective pedagogies of the state emerge – when education as a comfort zone for whiteness is disturbed.

As these examples demonstrate, the oscillation between a happy benevolent state and a wounded fragile state is used to defend whiteness, to secure its domination but also its comfort across public, social, political and everyday life. When these feeling-states are called into question – when their underpinning racism is named, when the comfortableness of whiteness is rattled – defensive and often violent responses ensue. These responses work as affective pedagogies, continually relaying and creating attachments to whiteness, attempting to teach the public what is acceptable, speakable and thinkable in the ongoing project of settler colonialism. This has the effect of securing a home for some whilst rendering others homeless. As the popular racist slogan goes, *if you don't love it then leave.*

The homeliness and homelessness of whiteness

Our discussions across this book have explored how denial, defensiveness and pride are active feeling-states in the production of white ignorance – shaping exclusions and distortions within school and university curricular reform and in the material cultures of schools: flag-flying, bicentenary celebrations and so on. The production of affect in the settler colonial state is thus vital for maintaining material and epistemological dominance. The redressal of racism in Australia calls for remaking affective relations – across public cultures, in interpersonal exchanges and within the institution of education itself. However, as Sara Ahmed describes, questions of justice are not simply about creating 'good feelings' or even about 'feeling better'.[73] Pedagogies that are *of* the settler state will always seek to comfort whiteness – to make it feel better in the face of its illegitimacy. A nation built on stolen land is constantly longing to feel at home. Indeed, the rage and fear expressed when whiteness is questioned demonstrates the anxiety and discomfort that is part of the ongoing desire for white possession and homeliness.[74]

The learned responses to these feeling-states of white woundedness and fragility can take many forms, rationalising everything from racist jokes and subtle put-downs, to school expulsions, violence, surveillance and incarceration. At its core, the wounded fragile state makes humanity conditional upon whiteness. The racialised Other is made less-than-human – their knowledges, histories, experiences, feelings, relationships, dignity and rights are pushed out of the frame. They are made homeless, dispossessed and expelled. Across public culture, political discourse and media commentary, the dehumanisation and expulsion of those who threaten whiteness is rife. Here, the victim of racism, when responding to it, is frequently made into a threat. This, we argue, is how the superiority of whiteness continues to be learned, aided by a pedagogy of the state in which media, politicians, public figures, industry leaders and ordinary citizens collectively defend the feeling-states of whiteness and, in so doing, position racialised Others as volatile and dangerous, as less-than-human. This is how Indigenous people, non-white migrants and people of colour in Australia become something for whiteness to control, contain and temper. They are made criminal and deviant against an imagined good and benevolent, though fragile and anxious, whiteness.

Pedagogies of the state teach the denial and suppression of difficult feelings that come with the past, present and futures of settler colonialism: unfamiliarity, discontinuity, fear, uncertainty, loss. It is through the constant deferral of these difficult feeling-states between individuals and institutions that the dominance of whiteness can continue. Instead, new affective relations need to be recognised and supported; educational relations that confront these affective attachments and divest from desires for white possession and dominance. This calls for sustained political work which takes active and always-discomforting account of the white supremacy and violence of the settler colonial state. Such work will require pedagogies through which whiteness can be collectively interrogated, to engage in processes of repair without absolution; pedagogies which can give rise to new restitutive and rectificatory material, epistemic and affective relations. These are the challenges that we turn to in Part III, to imagine an education for reparative futures.

PART III

OPENINGS

6
Educational Reckonings

We often expect that the conclusion of a book will attempt to resolve or reconcile its central problem. This is perhaps especially the case within the field of education, quite understandably so. Education is grounded in practice which has real effects on people's lives. Any critical interrogation of education systems, therefore, will compel questions of what should be done: how to 'fix' things, how to 'intervene', how to make it 'better'. As readers, we've sometimes been guilty of flicking straight to the closing pages of books such as this one, searching for signposts for action, hope or resolution. Maybe you are here now doing that very thing.

Unceded and unbroken Indigenous sovereignty and the very presence of non-white people, knowledges and histories have been recurring 'threats' to the white possessive of Australian settler colonialism. As we have explored in previous chapters, in the face of this perceived threat, education has been used time and again to secure the future of whiteness. Such educative efforts of the settler colonial state are therefore not only anxious and defensive projects, but are also ongoing. The aim of this concluding chapter is not to offer a template for response or a manual for change, but to reflect on how the injustices of learning whiteness that we have examined – across their material, epistemic and affective dimensions – call for far more expansive engagements with what education is and deep reckonings about what it can do to address racial violence. 'Reckoning requires everyday folks to bring about bold change', as Wiradjuri and Wailwan activist and author Teela Reid writes; '... it's time to show up'.[1]

And yet, discourses of education policy and reform are overwhelmingly preoccupied with questions of 'effectiveness', 'improvement' and, most recently during the pandemic, 'catch up'. These narrow framings arguably misrecognise, circumscribe or simplify problems within education and therefore delimit possibilities for its bold transformation.

Rarely do reform discourses see education in direct relation to the workings of the settler colonial state, its active historical legacies, its pedagogies in whiteness. As our analysis has attempted to make clear, policy treatments of education in the settler colony not only allow whiteness to perpetuate, but can also bolster it and position it as an inevitability. Tinkering at the edges, piecemeal interventions, or locating either blame or responsibility solely with individuals such as teachers and students are not merely insufficient as policy responses; such blinkered approaches also actively entrench education's complicities in racial violence.

The expansive conversations we are calling for, then, need to recognise and speak directly to the assumptive frameworks of whiteness in education – the entwined material, cognitive and affective economies of whiteness, its foundation in racial capitalism, its production of white ignorance, its feeling-states. That whiteness operates across all these dimensions, and that these dimensions themselves are interlocking and co-constitutive, is the key idea we wish to underline in this book. For example, whilst diversifying curricula is an important part of 'unlearning' whiteness, without associated moves to address the divisions in labour, extractions of value, or the affectations of the white nation, educational systems will ultimately remain steeped in racial domination.

This does not dismiss individual or institutional efforts to address racism, but calls for a deeper understanding of the contingencies of such efforts in order to guard against simplistic, tokenistic and harmful educational responses. Grappling with the complexity and pervasiveness of learning whiteness offers a better and necessarily more difficult starting point for reckoning with it. In other words, in bringing the material, the epistemic and the affective into a single analytic frame, we have sought to offer a more robust political perspective for addressing the structural formations of racial domination and the abiding logics of the white possessive in education.

We have not arrived: education beyond closure and redemption

We deliberately resist the impulse of closure here, the urge to find 'neat solutions' to a more complexly stated problem. Instead, we see the field of education as having an ongoing responsibility: to create and hold open spaces for grappling with the injustices of racism and settler colonialism; to cultivate relations of collective solidarity; to support an education that reckons with the past, present and futures of whiteness; and, as we shall discuss below, to do so without expecting redemption or prefiguring reconciliation.[2] Therefore, our focus in this chapter is not on how education can be 'improved' in the present or how it can 'move on' from its past, as dominant reform discourses would have it, but, rather, on how education can be reimagined to open up futures not structured by any form of racial domination. This is a reparatory project for education; an education that holds together the past, present and future in its difficult work to redress rather than reproduce injustices.

Here, we come back to a theme that we explored earlier in the book – the ever-present hope and violence of education. Our critique of education's role in sustaining whiteness does not lead us to a position of being 'against' education as such. Indeed educative projects have been central to some of the most important refusals of whiteness, from fugitive pedagogies and movements to decolonise the curriculum, to Indigenous-led calls for truth telling. As Paul Gilroy reflects, there is much to be learned from such active histories of rebellion and dissidence against racial domination.[3] These are not lessons that exist to extract from suffering or make harms 'worthwhile'. Nor are they lessons by which to circumscribe the lives of Indigenous people and people of colour, as if these lives have no meaning beyond negation and reaction against white supremacy. Equally important here is the recognition of all that which makes for flourishing and joy. Such active histories of struggle and creativity, Gilroy suggests, can furnish resources that, if listened to and acted upon with humility, can guide a *collective* pursuit of justice. The building of new relations of education and transgressive modes of learning across these histories of struggle points to the simple and yet *vital* idea that it is possible to live and think otherwise.

This expression of hope in the idea of education – if not in its present dominant forms – is not the stuff of white optimism. We do not seek to lay empty claims to ideas of 'progress' and 'fairness', as has been done so often through liberal gestures that, in fact, uphold racial orders.[4] Instead, in order to imagine and engage a different future, hope might be better derived from an ongoing acknowledgement of education's past and present violence. For, divesting from whiteness – actively unlearning it – cannot proceed through the kinds of denials and distortions that are permitted when history is cleaved from the yet-to-come. This is to say, there is an ongoing need to hold in tension, and be deeply conscious of, the past that endures in the present as much as there is a need to hold in tension, and work actively with, the capacity of education to be hopeful *and* violent. Such attentiveness to the contingencies of education against the structures of history does not shut down the possibilities of change or the chances for agency. For neither the idea of education nor the possibilities for the future are foreclosed; they are sites of continual struggle and, just as there is no end to history, they cannot be definitively bounded or prefigured. This is why we have called this 'concluding' section of the book 'openings'.

Indeed, grappling with these tensions in education raises complex issues of responsibility and complicity which work in different ways across institutions, individual action, communities and social and economic structures. In this book we've explored how whiteness is learned through the active pedagogies of the settler colonial state; whiteness is not a natural nor an innocent social order – it is continually made, recalibrated, relayed and learned in material, epistemic and affective ways. Thus, *un*learning whiteness – divesting from it in all its educational forms – also calls for active, intentional and structural responses. As we set out at the start of this book, the three of us write from 'within' the systems we are troubled by. In different ways we are thoroughly enmeshed in learning whiteness: as settlers, parents, teachers, workers, consumers, and across our varying class locations and racialised positions. From where we send our own children to school to our roles within elite universities, we participate in educational systems that uphold white supremacy. We have our own blind spots, contradictions, complicities. As individuals we often fail in dinting, let alone dismantling, the structures of whiteness that we've identified in the previous pages of this book.

The perceived limits of individual action, however, ought not to give air to settler narcissistic guilt or what Alexis Shotwell calls the 'purity politics of despair'.[5] As Aziz Choudry reflects, while 'we live, learn and organize in a web of contradictions', we do not have to foreclose possibilities for solidarity or shut down ways of collectively reimagining what else might be possible.[6] For settlers such as ourselves, there is an ongoing responsibility to understand how the settler colonial state works on each of us differently, shaping the material, cognitive and affective economies of our lives, precisely so that we can find and *persist with* ways to disrupt its logics. In the words of First Nations legal scholar Irene Watson: 'it is in thinking through how to engage with Aboriginal sovereignties that Australian society in the main becomes "stuck", where the ground of "impossibility" lies, but it is this ground "exactly" where our thinking should begin'.[7] Watson offers a profound reframing of the project of education. Rather than learning whiteness, learning the *contingencies* of whiteness in the settler colony – its historical conditions into the present – can create new conditions of possibility: 'to engage with thinking beyond the impossible'.[8] People have always navigated, refused and attempted to undo and escape systems of oppression; history is testament to the possibility of agency, and it is precisely the possibility of agency that makes futures – even if we are not able to name these futures yet. Lessons in the futurity of whiteness can be interrogated and rescripted, not simply assimilated and imbibed.

The political work of this book, if partial and modest, lies in its documenting of the materialities, knowledges and feelings of whiteness precisely to remind us of the possibilities to learn otherwise.

Unlearning whiteness

all the things that are next
lives within
the hearts
minds
hopes
of Indigenous peoples
and of Settlers
who are committed
to justice

From 'Futures' by Ambelin Kwaymullina, 2021[9]

Palyku novelist and academic Ambelin Kwaymullina offers in her book *Living on Stolen Land* some pathways towards a decolonised future. She asks settlers to be attentive to relations of learning, to listen and act with humility, and to be grounded in respect for Indigenous people and Indigenous sovereignty.[10] She underlines the importance of ongoing processes of respectful, relational and responsive responsibility (the 'how'), and not just claims to pre-fixed outcomes or initiatives (the 'what'). And, as the words above from her poem 'Futures' invoke, this is a commitment requiring connection – of both ideas and people – to remake nothing short of the social contract. Thinking with Kwaymullina's words, we consider how the relationship between education and the future might be recast.

Indeed, this is a relationship that is often taken for granted. As Keri Facer has recently written, 'As politicians and singers constantly remind us: "children are the future". From this assumption spring political promises to create "schools for tomorrow", to invest in education "for the future", and prepare young people for a "world yet to come".'[11] But there is a need to better understand these assumptions; ideas of the future in education wield immense power – justifying transformations of everyday life, shaping education and action in the present. '*How* we think about ideas of the future in education therefore matters not because "education is the future", or because "education shapes the future", but because these ideas fundamentally shape what we think education is and can be today.'[12]

Facer's examination of the different ideas of the future in education has shown that mainstream education policy the world over has been preoccupied with how education can best 'prepare' students for the future.[13] As a dominant orientation, 'education as preparation for the future' foregrounds instrumentality and a fixed sense of 'the what'. Implied here is that the future can be prefigured and known; a particular future scenario is presented of, for example, economic change or technological disruption, and the goal of education is to equip students to manage in that world.[14] We see this when education is positioned in terms of workforce planning or national development, or, as in Frydenberg's words at the very start of this book, in terms of being a 'first defence' of the state. Such models of 'education as preparation' become sites for the exercise of power. As Facer argues, 'those who are able to claim "knowledge" of the future are able to claim authority over the practice of education in the present'.[15]

We suggest here that the white possessive attempts to claim not only the materialities, knowledges and feelings of the settler colonial state, but also the very idea of the future itself.[16] Whiteness, Andrew Baldwin reflects, 'has a stake in the future'; its very logic is to maintain and accumulate its perceived value and power over time.[17] The public – young and old alike – are asked to accept and prepare for a future of undisturbed white domination.[18] As *Learning Whiteness* has demonstrated, the continuity of settler occupation and white dominance into the future is *actively* taught and defended through the pedagogies of the state. What needs to happen today to create futures that are not structured by whiteness? How can the material, epistemic and affective harms and injustices of the past and present be recognised and reckoned with to open up futures of justice and dignity? What kinds of refusals and abolitions are necessary for – as scholars grappling with the violence of settler colonialism and advanced capitalism in other parts of the world suggest – 'hospicing the old world and curating the decay of harmful structures'?[19] In the long process of writing this book we have come to these questions in different ways and struggled together about how we might respond. But just as these provocations take on different meanings in our different contexts and lives, we expect they do too for readers. Filling possibility with specificity is precisely the ongoing work of unlearning whiteness, the 'how' rather than the 'what', fraught and incomplete as it is.

A point of entry we offer, then, starts from acknowledging the need to challenge at every turn any concept of the future within education that prefigures the white possessive. Within education there are, as Facer puts it, 'injustices upon which futures are being envisaged'.[20] There is, at the same time, a potential for education systems and practices to grapple squarely with these injustices, inviting a different construction of the relationship between education and the future. As one of us (Arathi) has explored with colleagues, this relationship could be one guided by ideas of reparation:

> The idea of reparative futures signals a commitment to identify and recognise the injustices visited on, and experienced by, individuals and communities in the past. It understands that these past injustices, even when they appear to be distant in time or 'over', will continue

> to endure in people's lives in material and affective ways unless, and until, they are consciously and carefully addressed.[21]

The lens of reparations here opens up new possible futures rather than seeking an ending or a simplistic 'repair' of history. In this sense, education for reparative futures implies an ongoing and perhaps never 'settled' commitment to reconstruct relations oriented towards justice.

Indeed, there are two ideas present in this work on reparative futures in education which seem particularly relevant to our discussions on whiteness. First, the past, present and future are brought together – their relationships are necessarily entwined within the pursuit of justice. This offers a challenge to dominant preparatory models of education which prefigure the futurity of capitalism and colonialism – and with that, whiteness – and which attempt to secure it through separating or weakening historical connections: reasserting a selective version of the past (for example, in terms of school curricula or national celebrations), or turning away from the active histories of settler colonialism altogether (for example, when educational disparities are explained by the 'nature' of specific groups). As Charles W. Mills has examined, the structural injustice of whiteness is able to persist by rendering calls for any kind of rectificatory justice as permanently *untimely* – erased from empirical, theoretical and moral considerations, both today and tomorrow.[22] This is why, as we have explored throughout this book, understanding the entanglement of the past-present-future of whiteness – its modes of possession, accumulation and expansion across time – is central to reckoning with it.

Second, the idea of reparative futures in education acknowledges that injustices work across material, epistemic and affective domains. As our analysis of learning whiteness has shown, these are, in fact, not separate but co-articulating forces in social life. Thus, an education for unlearning whiteness and for reparative futures can invite us to address each of these domains, as well as their complexities and interconnections. For example, our analyses of the materialities of learning whiteness demonstrated how systems of valorisation – with their hierarchic rendering of life – are produced through the enclosures/dispossessions and divided labours of education. A process for reparative redress could explore material restitutions for these dehumanising economies of whiteness. It could see things like land back movements, restitution of resources and the abolition of violent systems of racial capitalism, first, as possible, and second, as central to the project of education itself – both within institutions and across public pedagogies. It could recognise that exhortations for greater commitments to 'public' education or 'diversity' and 'inclusion' cannot occur without such material transformations, without divesting from the material futures of whiteness.

Shaping these material possibilities are matters of knowledge. For, crucial to working out the process and nature of material reparation is an ethics of listening and dialogue that is capable of generating new perspectives and action, based on a commitment to understand and be in solidarity with Indigenous sovereignties and lifeworlds, as well as with the lived experiences of people of colour under systems of racial domination. This necessarily involves decentring the forms and practices of knowledge that have upheld epistemic injustices, that have dehumanised non-white people by denying their epistemic capacity and authority. It would entail a process of cultivating spaces for reparative remembering, as well as resources for collaboratively interpreting histories and experiences of settler state violence and creating the means to work through them.[23] These are, fundamentally, relations of learning that can, do and should take place through education, within, against and beyond institutions.[24] Indeed, the material significance of the epistemic has been closely understood within anti-colonial and anti-racist movements, as our discussions of truth telling and decolonising the curriculum in earlier chapters explored. The shared responsibility of questioning the power relations of knowledge and interrogating material and affective investments in white ignorance – of listening more carefully, honouring silences and fostering new ways of knowing – offer openings for epistemic reparation.

These epistemic shifts can be difficult and discomforting precisely because the project of learning whiteness is deeply affective. An education that is committed to unlearning whiteness and working for reparative futures would need to foster means of understanding how, first, systems of racial domination work upon all our lives; second, how we are each positioned in different ways in and through these histories; and third, how we all have affective capacities that can move us towards a collective pursuit of racial justice. 'How' this occurs, to reflect again on Ambelin Kwaymullina's words, is a critical consideration in shaping the pedagogies for reparative futures – within classrooms, families, workplaces and public discourse. It would involve creating openings which critically respond to, rather than accept, the defensiveness and backlashes of whiteness; which would proceed from the recognition of Indigenous sovereignty and find ways to question and rupture assertions of the settler state's assumed benevolence; and which would understand the ongoing harms of whiteness and actively seek means for repair and restitution.

These commitments require taking seriously the discomforts which are sometimes personal and sometimes institutional, but which are always needed to disrupt the homeliness of whiteness. Such discomforts are an opportunity for establishing different relations, not for defensive or retreating responses. These relational, affective orientations have material effects because they create new feeling-states around which social and political futures might be arranged. In this work, settler and white feelings of redemption or closure, or a desire for 'reconciliation', are inadequate for – and often obstructive to – unlearning whiteness and creating reparative futures. Those are, after all, the feeling-states that keep the structures of whiteness – white ownership of the future – in place.[25]

An education for reparative futures, then, is open to the possibility that the settler state as we know it, with its current logics of the white possessive, could cease to exist. This is not, historically speaking, inconceivable and, moreover, for the imagination of a just future, it is a necessary possibility. But it is the very potential of a radically different future for Australia that drives ever more defensive and fearful pedagogies of the state. Arguably, ideas of Indigenous sovereignty, Indigenous self-determination and futures beyond whiteness incite backlash and fear because it is assumed such futures will invert racial domination rather than destroy it. Perhaps the most dangerous project of learning whiteness is that it forestalls and obstructs the potential for a capacious humanism, radical in its commitment to racial justice. Thus, it follows that the most important lesson for unlearning whiteness is that a future divested from racial domination is not a foreclosed future; it is one open to the fullness of human dignity, flourishing and possibility.

Notes

Chapter 1

1. Dujuan Hoosan, 'I Am Cheeky, But No Kid Should Be in Jail. This Is Why I Addressed the UN at Just 12 Years Old', *Guardian*, 11 September 2019, http://www.theguardian.com/commentisfree/2019/sep/12/i-am-cheeky-but-no-kid-should-be-in-jail-this-is-why-i-addressed-the-un-at-just-12-years-old.
2. Josh Frydenberg, 'Treasurer Josh Frydenberg's 2019 Budget Speech – in Full', *Guardian*, 2 April 2019, http://www.theguardian.com/australia-news/2019/apr/02/treasurer-josh-frydenbergs-2019-budget-speech-in-full.
3. Throughout this book we use a range of terms that refer to the sovereign first peoples of what is now Australia. For collective signification we use Indigenous, First Nations and Aboriginal and Torres Strait Islander people. Sometimes Aboriginal is used to indicate both Aboriginal and Torres Strait Islander. These terms are all imposed and inadequate but are what we have to work with when wishing to discuss collective Indigenous experiences, issues or concerns. Where possible we also refer to specific First Nations groups. We do this in relation to particular examples and to scholars who identify with particular Aboriginal or Torres Strait Islander groups. Sometimes these names will have multiple spellings. See also Luke Pearson's examination of the politics of naming and the responsibilities non-Indigenous, settler people have to respectful naming and communication: 'Appropriate Terminology for Aboriginal and Torres Strait Islander People – It's Complicated', *IndigenousX*, 16 June 2021, https://indigenousx.com.au/appropriate-terminology-for-aboriginal-and-torres-strait-islander-people-its-complicated.
4. Aileen Moreton-Robinson, *The White Possessive: Property, Power, and Indigenous Sovereignty* (Minneapolis: University of Minnesota

Press, 2015). Moreton-Robinson's extensive writings on the white possessive logics of settler colonialism also include: 'Virtuous Racial States', *Griffith Law Review* 20, no. 3 (1 January 2011): 641–58, and 'Incommensurable Sovereignties', in *Routledge Handbook of Critical Indigenous Studies*, ed. Brendan Hokowhitu, Aileen Moreton-Robinson, Linda Tuhiwai-Smith, Chris Andersen and Steve Larkin (Abingdon: Routledge, 2020), 257–68.

5. Moreton-Robinson, 'Incommensurable Sovereignties'.
6. Moreton-Robinson, *The White Possessive*.
7. Michelle Bishop, 'A Rationale for the Urgency of Indigenous Education Sovereignty: Enough's Enough', *The Australian Educational Researcher* 48, no. 3 (1 July 2021): 421.
8. While it is often easier to write about these interlocking forces by separating them, we are attempting to hold such tensions together, and to point to and emphasise intersections and interdependencies, even while the written form may ultimately fail us in completely realising this goal.
9. See Fazal Rizvi, 'Children and the Grammar of Popular Racism', in *Race, Identity and Representation in Education*, ed. Cameron McCarthy, Warren Crichlow, Greg Dimitriadis and Nadine Dolby (New York: Routledge, 2005). In this work, Rizvi explores how everyday cultural practices of representation in Australian primary schools create racist ideas of social difference. Drawing on Stuart Hall, he calls these practices the 'grammars' of popular racism.
10. On the idea of 'connected sociology', which seeks to reconstruct historically interlinked understandings of the social world, see Gurminder Bhambra, *Connected Sociologies* (London: Bloomsbury, 2014).
11. See, for example, Hamid Dabashi, 'Black Lives Matter and Palestine: A Historic Alliance', Al Jazeera, 6 September 2016, https://www.aljazeera.com/opinions/2016/9/6/black-lives-matter-and-palestine-a-historic-alliance; Cristina Verán, 'Black Lives Matter: Indigenous Australia's Solidarity with the U.S. Movement for Black Lives', *Cultural Survival Quarterly Magazine*, September 2020, https://www.culturalsurvival.org/publications/cultural-survival-quarterly/blak-lives-matter-indigenous-australias-solidarity-us.

12. Ambelin Kwaymullina, *Living on Stolen Land* (Broome, Western Australia: Magabala Books, 2020), 55.
13. For discussion of the transnational development of white supremacist extremism see The Soufan Center, 'White Supremacy Extremism: The Transnational Rise of the Violent White Supremacist Movement', 27 September 2019, https://thesoufancenter.org/research/white-supremacy-extremism-the-transnational-rise-of-the-violent-white-supremacist-movement.
14. Greg Barton, 'To Shut Down Far-Right Extremism in Australia, We Must Confront the Ecosystem of Hate', *The Conversation*, 7 February 2021, http://theconversation.com/to-shut-down-far-right-extremism-in-australia-we-must-confront-the-ecosystem-of-hate-154269.
15. Kathomi Gatwiri and Leticia Anderson, 'The Senate Has Voted to Reject Critical Race Theory from the National Curriculum. What Is It, and Why Does It Matter?', *The Conversation*, 22 June 2021, http://theconversation.com/the-senate-has-voted-to-reject-critical-race-theory-from-the-national-curriculum-what-is-it-and-why-does-it-matter-163102.
16. Amanda Porter and Eddie Cubillo, 'Not Criminals or Passive Victims: Media Need to Reframe Their Representation of Aboriginal Deaths in Custody', *The Conversation*, 20 April 2021, http://theconversation.com/not-criminals-or-passive-victims-media-need-to-reframe-their-representation-of-aboriginal-deaths-in-custody-158561.
17. Lorena Allam, Calla Wahlquist, Nick Evershed and Miles Herbert, 'The 474 Deaths Inside: Tragic Toll of Indigenous Deaths in Custody Revealed', *Guardian*, 8 April 2021, http://www.theguardian.com/australia-news/2021/apr/09/the-474-deaths-inside-rising-number-of-indigenous-deaths-in-custody-revealed.
18. Government of Canada, Royal Canadian Mounted Police, 'Missing and Murdered Aboriginal Women: A National Operational Overview', 27 May 2014, https://www.rcmp-grc.gc.ca/en/missing-and-murdered-aboriginal-women-national-operational-overview.
19. On anti-Palestinian racism under settler colonialism, see Ghada Karmi, 'The Conflict in the Middle East Is Sustained by the

Silencing of Palestinians', *Guardian*, 10 June 2021, http://www.theguardian.com/commentisfree/2021/jun/10/conflict-middle-east-silencing-palestinians-rights. On the complex working of whiteness and settler colonialism in Israel, see Noura Erakat, 'Whiteness as Property in Israel: Revival, Rehabilitation, and Removal', *Harvard Journal on Racial & Ethnic Justice* 69 (5 July 2015): 1–36.

20. Sara Ahmed, 'Multiculturalism and the Promise of Happiness', *New Formations*, no. 63 (2007): 121–38.
21. As we will discuss in Chapter 4, all school children in Australia were given a 'bicentenary coin' in 1988 to 'celebrate' 200 years of British occupation and the settler colonial nation.
22. Shino Konishi, 'First Nations Scholars, Settler Colonial Studies, and Indigenous History', *Australian Historical Studies* 50, no. 3 (3 July 2019): 20.
23. Konishi, 'First Nations Scholars', 9.
24. Jessica Pykett, 'Citizenship Education and Narratives of Pedagogy', *Citizenship Studies* 14, no. 6 (1 December 2010): 623.
25. See also on pedagogies of the state, Arathi Sriprakash, Peter Sutoris and Kevin Myers, 'The Science of Childhood and the Pedagogy of the State: Postcolonial Development in India, 1950s', *Journal of Historical Sociology* 32, no. 3 (2019): 345–59.
26. See, for example, Gabrielle Appleby and Megan Davis, 'The Uluru Statement and the Promises of Truth', *Australian Historical Studies* 49, no. 4 (2 October 2018): 501–9; the National Indigenous Youth Education Coalition's Learn Our Truth campaign, https://www.niyec.com/learn-our-truth; Emma Masters, 'Growing Number of Aboriginal Communities Setting Up Independent Schools to Teach "Both Ways"', ABC News (Australia), 3 July 2021, https://www.abc.net.au/news/2021-07-04/teaching-blends-aboriginal-culture-language-western-numeracy/100237208; Amy Claire Thomas, 'Bilingual Education, Aboriginal Self-Determination and Yolngu Control of Shepherdson College, 1972-1983', *History of Education Review* 50, no. 2 (2021): 196–211.
27. Leigh Patel, 'Fugitive Practices: Learning in a Settler Colony', *Educational Studies* 55, no. 3 (2019): 257. The idea of 'fugitive pedagogy' has also been developed in Jarvis R. Givens, *Fugitive*

Pedagogy: Carter G. Woodson and the Art of Black Teaching (Cambridge, MA: Harvard University Press, 2021). Examining the ideas and work of Black educators in the USA in the twentieth century, Givens argues that 'fugitive pedagogy' isn't merely an elaborate metaphor, but a set of practices rooted in the physical and intellectual life of Black people under slavery and its afterlives. For discussions about learning beyond institutions in the Australian settler colony see Wayne Atkinson, 'The Schools of Human Experience', in *First Australians*, ed. Rachel Perkins and Marcia Langton (Carlton, Vic: The Miegunyah Press, 2010), 185–216; Sophie Rudolph, 'Demanding Dialogue in an Unsettled Settler State: Implications for Education and Justice'. *History of Education Review* 50, no. 2 (2021): 181–95.

28. Martin Nakata, *Disciplining the Savages, Savaging the Disciplines* (Canberra: Aboriginal Studies Press, 2007); Martin Nakata, 'The Cultural Interface', *The Australian Journal of Indigenous Education* 36 (2007): 7–14.
29. Martin Nakata, Victoria Nakata, Sarah Keech and Reuben Bolt, 'Decolonial Goals and Pedagogies for Indigenous Studies', *Decolonization: Indigeneity, Education & Society* 1, no. 1 (2012). See also Nikki Moodie, 'Learning about Knowledge: Threshold Concepts for Indigenous Studies in Education', *The Australian Educational Researcher* 46, no. 5 (1 March 2019): 735–49.

Chapter 2

1. Rebecca Urban, 'National Curriculum: Christian Heritage Sacrificed in School Shake-up', *The Australian*, 29 April 2021, behind paywall at https://tinyurl.com/ywa23yat. We discuss the active sponsorship of 'Western civilisation' in education in Chapter 4.
2. See Patrick Wolfe, 'Land, Labor, and Difference: Elementary Structures of Race', *The American Historical Review*, no. 3 (2001): 866–905; Michael Omi and Howard Winant, *Racial Formation in the United States* [1986] (New York: Routledge, 2014); Aileen Moreton-Robinson, ed., *Whitening Race: Essays in Social and Cultural Criticism* (Canberra: Aboriginal Studies Press, 2011).

3. Sara Ahmed, 'A Phenomenology of Whiteness', *Feminist Theory* 8, no. 2 (2007): 149–68.
4. David Theo Goldberg, *The Racial State* (Oxford: Blackwell, 2002), 173.
5. On the malleability of whiteness see, for example, Michelle Christian, 'A Global Critical Race and Racism Framework: Racial Entanglements and Deep and Malleable Whiteness', *Sociology of Race and Ethnicity* 5, no. 2 (2019): 169–85; Riyad A. Shahjahan and Kirsten T. Edwards, 'Whiteness as Futurity and Globalization of Higher Education', *Higher Education* (2021): 1–18, https://doi.org/10.1007/s10734-021-00702-x.
6. Goldberg, *The Racial State*, 176.
7. Moreton-Robinson, *The White Possessive.*
8. Moodie, 'Learning about Knowledge', 740.
9. See, for example, Karim Murji and John Solomos, *Racialization: Studies in Theory and Practice* (Oxford: Oxford University Press, 2005).
10. Moodie, 'Learning about Knowledge', 740.
11. Lisa Tilley and Robbie Shilliam, *Raced Markets: An Introduction* (Abingdon: Taylor & Francis, 2018), 534.
12. Nelson Maldonado-Torres argues that the project of sixteenth-century European colonisation of the Americas became a *model* of power, creating 'a widespread and general attitude regarding the humanity of colonized and enslaved subjects' that forged colonial projects in others sites and times. See Nelson Maldonado-Torres, 'On the Coloniality of Being: Contributions to the Development of a Concept', *Cultural Studies* 21, no. 2–3 (2007): 244.
13. Cedric J. Robinson, *Black Marxism: The Making of the Black Radical Tradition* (Chapel Hill: University of North Carolina Press, 2000), 9.
14. Robinson, *Black Marxism*, 26.
15. Robinson, *Black Marxism*, 26.
16. Robinson, *Black Marxism*, 27.
17. W.E.B. Du Bois, *The Souls of Black Folk* [1903] (Oxford: Oxford University Press, 2007).

18. W.E.B. Du Bois, 'The Souls of White Folk', *The Independent* (USA), 10 August 1910. Reprinted in W.E.B. Du Bois, *Writings* (New York: Library of America, 1987), 924.
19. Du Bois, 'The Souls of White Folk', 924.
20. Marilyn Lake and Henry Reynolds, *Drawing the Global Colour Line: White Men's Countries and the Question of Racial Equality* (Carlton: Melbourne University Publishing, 2008), 3; see also Bill Schwarz, *The White Man's World: Memories of Empire* (Oxford: Oxford University Press, 2011).
21. Du Bois, 'The Souls of White Folk', 924.
22. Aníbal Quijano, 'Coloniality and Modernity/Rationality', *Cultural Studies* 21, no. 2–3 (2007): 168.
23. Maldonado-Torres, 'Coloniality of Being', 243. On the entangled histories of colonialism see, for example, Simon J. Potter and Jonathan Saha, 'Global History, Imperial History and Connected Histories of Empire', *Journal of Colonialism and Colonial History* 16, no. 1 (2015); Eliga H. Gould, 'Entangled Histories, Entangled Worlds: The English-Speaking Atlantic as a Spanish Periphery', *The American Historical Review* 112, no. 3 (2007): 764–86.
24. Patrick Wolfe, 'Settler Colonialism and the Elimination of the Native', *Journal of Genocide Research* 8, no. 4 (December 2006): 387–409.
25. Maldonado-Torres, 'Coloniality of Being', 243.
26. Quijano, 'Coloniality and Modernity/Rationality'.
27. Moreton-Robinson, *The White Possessive*, xix (emphasis added).
28. Moreton-Robinson, *The White Possessive*, 66, 157.
29. Goldberg, *The Racial State*, 4.
30. Goldberg, *The Racial State*, 175.
31. Goldberg, *The Racial State*, 140.
32. Moreton-Robinson, *The White Possessive*, 177.
33. Moreton-Robinson, 'Virtuous Racial States', 647.
34. Moreton-Robinson, 'Virtuous Racial States', 647.
35. Ghassan Hage, *White Nation: Fantasies of White Supremacy in a Multicultural Nation* [1998] (London: Routledge, 2000).
36. Hage, *White Nation*, 18.

37. Roland Bleiker, David Campbell, Emma Hutchison and Xzarina Nicholson, 'The Visual Dehumanisation of Refugees', *Australian Journal of Political Science* 48, no. 4 (2013): 398–416.
38. Patrick Barkham, 'Australia Votes on How Tightly to Close the Door', *Guardian*, 10 November 2001, http://www.theguardian.com/world/2001/nov/10/immigration.uk; 'Truth Overboard – The Story That Won't Go Away', *Sydney Morning Herald*, 28 February 2006, https://www.smh.com.au/national/truth-overboard-the-story-that-wont-go-away-20060228-gdn224.html. See also Kate Slattery, 'Drowning Not Waving: The "Children Overboard" Event and Australia's Fear of the Other', *Media International Australia* 109, no. 1 (2003): 93–108.
39. Moreton-Robinson, *The White Possessive*, xxiv.
40. Debbie Bargallie, *Unmasking the Racial Contract: Indigenous Voices on Racism in the Australian Public Service* (Canberra: Aboriginal Studies Press, 2020).
41. Moreton-Robinson, 'Virtuous Racial States', 646.
42. Goldberg, *The Racial State*, 104.
43. Audra Simpson, *Mohawk Interruptus* (Durham, NC: Duke University Press, 2014), 116.
44. Christian, 'A Global Critical Race and Racism Framework', 170.
45. Cheryl Harris, 'Whiteness as Property', *Harvard Law Review* 106, no. 8 (1993): 1707–91.
46. Harris, 'Whiteness as Property', 1714.
47. Harris, 'Whiteness as Property', 1734.
48. Moreton-Robinson, *The White Possessive*, xix (emphasis added).
49. Eve Tuck and K. Wayne Yang, 'Decolonization Is Not a Metaphor', *Decolonization: Indigeneity, Education & Society* 1, no. 1 (2012): 5.
50. Fiona Nicoll, 'Reconciliation in and out of Perspective: White Knowing, Seeing, Curating and Being at Home in and against Indigenous Sovereignty', in *Whitening Race*, ed. Moreton-Robinson, 17–31.
51. Ghassan Hage, *Is Racism an Environmental Threat?* (Cambridge: Polity, 2017), 94.
52. Shannon Sullivan, 'White World-Traveling', *The Journal of Speculative Philosophy* 18, no. 4 (2004): 302.

53. Alison Whittaker, 'So White. So What', *Meanjin*, Autumn 2020, https://meanjin.com.au/essays/so-white-so-what.
54. Helen Ngo, *The Habits of Racism: A Phenomenology of Racism and Racialized Embodiment* (Lanham: Lexington Books, 2017).
55. Ahmed, 'A Phenomenology of Whiteness'.
56. On the white ontological expansiveness of 'inclusion' projects in UK universities, see Sharon Walker, 'Whiteness and Exclusion: An Ethnography of the Racialised Discourse of the UK's Widening Participation Agenda' (Unpublished PhD Thesis, University of Cambridge, 2021).
57. Charles W. Mills, 'White Ignorance', in *Race and Epistemologies of Ignorance*, ed. Shannon Sullivan and Nancy Tuana (New York: State University of New York Press, 2007), 29. On the racial 'fantasies' of the Australian settler colony, see Hage, *White Nation.*
58. Elizabeth Jelin, *State Repression and the Labors of Memory* (Minneapolis: University of Minnesota Press, 2003), 5.
59. Ahmed, 'A Phenomenology of Whiteness', 154.
60. Harry Blagg and Thalia Anthony, '"Stone Walls Do Not a Prison Make": Bare Life and the Carceral Archipelago in Colonial and Postcolonial Societies', in *Human Rights and Incarceration: Critical Explorations*, ed. Elizabeth Stanley (Cham: Springer International, 2018), 261 (original emphasis); on the incarceration and policing of Indigenous girls in Canada see Jaskiran K. Dhillon, 'Indigenous Girls and the Violence of Settler Colonial Policing', *Decolonization: Indigeneity, Education & Society* 4, no. 2 (17 December 2015): 1–31.
61. Fadak Alfayadh, 'Dismantling the Detention Industrial Complex', in *Incarceration, Migration and Indigenous Sovereignty: Thoughts on Existence and Resistance in Racist Times*, ed. Holly Randell-Moon (Dunedin: Space, Race, Bodies; Department of Media, Film & Communication, University of Otago, 2017), 23–5.
62. Randa Abdel-Fattah, *Coming of Age in the War on Terror* (Sydney: New South Publishing, 2021).
63. Avneet Arora, 'Australia Announces Changes to Citizenship Test and English Language Program for Migrants', *SBS Your Language*, https://www.sbs.com.au/language/english/australia-announces-changes-to-citizenship-test-and-english-language-program-for-migrants.

64. Alfred and Corntassel discuss colonial power as a shape-shifter: 'the instruments of domination are evolving and inventing new methods to erase Indigenous histories and senses of place' (601). Taiaiake Alfred and Jeff Corntassel, 'Being Indigenous: Resurgences against Contemporary Colonialism', *Government and Opposition* 40, no. 4 (2005): 597–614.
65. See Zeus Leonardo, 'The Color of Supremacy: Beyond the Discourse of "White Privilege"', *Educational Philosophy and Theory* 36, no. 2 (2004): 137–52; Mills, 'White Ignorance'.
66. Jessica Pykett, 'Citizenship Education and Narratives of Pedagogy', *Citizenship Studies* 14, no. 6 (2010): 624.
67. Frydenberg, 'Treasurer Josh Frydenberg's 2019 budget speech – in full'.
68. Whittaker, 'So White. So What'.
69. Zsuzsa Millei, 'Pedagogy of Nation: A Concept and Method to Research Nationalism in Young Children's Institutional Lives', *Childhood* 26, no. 1 (2019): 84.
70. Julia Paulson, Nelson Abiti, Julian Bermeo Osorio, Carlos Arturo Charria Hernández, Duong Keo, Peter Manning, Lizzi O. Milligan, Kate Moles, Catriona Pennell and Sangar Salih, 'Education as Site of Memory: Developing a Research Agenda', *International Studies in Sociology of Education* 29, no. 4 (2020): 429–51.
71. Paulson et al., 'Education as Site of Memory', 433.

Chapter 3

1. Sharon Stein, 'Navigating Different Theories of Change for Higher Education in Volatile Times', *Educational Studies* 55, no. 6 (2019): 679.
2. Some of the ideas we develop in this chapter are drawn from Jessica Gerrard, Arathi Sriprakash and Sophie Rudolph, 'Education and Racial Capitalism', *Race, Ethnicity and Education* (2021), https://doi.org/10.1080/13613324.2021.2001449.
3. Onur Ulas Ince, *Colonial Capitalism and the Dilemmas of Liberalism* (Oxford: Oxford University Press, 2018), 4.

4. Moreton-Robinson, *The White Possessive*; Wahneema H. Lubiano, ed., *The House That Race Built: Black Americans, U.S. Terrain* (New York: Pantheon Books, 1997).
5. Satnam Virdee, 'Racialized Capitalism: An Account of Its Contested Origins and Consolidation', *The Sociological Review* 67, no. 1 (2019): 9.
6. Arun Kundnani, 'What Is Racial Capitalism?', Arun Kundnani: On Race, Culture, and Empire blog, 23 October 2020, https://www.kundnani.org/what-is-racial-capitalism.
7. Ben Silverstein, 'Reading Sovereignties in the Shadow of Settler Colonialism: Chinese Employment of Aboriginal Labour in the Northern Territory of Australia', *Postcolonial Studies* 23, no. 1 (2020): 43–57; Julia Martinez and Claire Lowrie, 'Colonial Constructions of Masculinity: Transforming Aboriginal Australian Men into "Houseboys"', *Gender & History* 21, no. 2 (2009): 305–23; Ann Curthoys and Clive Moore, 'Working for the White People: An Historiographic Essay on Aboriginal and Torres Strait Islander Labour', *Labour History*, no. 69 (1995): 1–29; Dawn May, 'The Articulation of the Aboriginal and Capitalist Modes on the North Queensland Pastoral Frontier', *Journal of Australian Studies* 7, no. 12 (1983): 34–44; Mark Hannah, 'Aboriginal Workers in the Australian Agricultural Company, 1824–1857', *Labour History* 82 (2002): 17–33.
8. Minoru Hokari, 'From Wattie Creek to Wattie Creek: An Oral Historical Approach to the Gurindji Walk-Off', *Aboriginal History* 24 (2000): 98–116.
9. Harris, 'Whiteness as Property'; Brenna Bhandar, *Colonial Lives of Property* (Durham, NC: Duke University Press, 2018); Moreton-Robinson, *The White Possessive*.
10. Robinson, *Black Marxism*.
11. Robinson, *Black Marxism*, 2.
12. Gargi Bhattacharyya, *Rethinking Racial Capitalism: Questions of Reproduction and Survival* (London: Rowman & Littlefield, 2018), x.
13. Karl Marx, *Capital, Vol. 1* (Chicago: University of Chicago Press, 1952), 377; see also Virdee, 'Racialized Capitalism'.

14. Jodi Melamed, 'Racial Capitalism', *Critical Ethnic Studies* 1, no. 1 (2015): 77.
15. Saidiya V. Hartman, *Scenes of Subjection: Terror, Slavery, and Self-Making in Nineteenth-Century America* (Oxford: Oxford University Press, 1997); Ruth Wilson Gilmore, *Golden Gulag: Prisons, Surplus, Crisis, and Opposition in Globalizing California* (Berkeley: University of California Press, 2007).
16. Sara Ahmed, *What's the Use? On the Uses of Use* (Durham, NC: Duke University Press, 2019), 95.
17. Jodi Melamed, *Represent and Destroy: Rationalizing Violence in the New Racial Capitalism* (Minneapolis: University of Minnesota Press, 2011).
18. See, for example, Arathi Sriprakash, Leon Tikly and Sharon Walker, 'The Erasures of Racism in Education and International Development: Re-Reading the "Global Learning Crisis"', *Compare: A Journal of Comparative and International Education* 50, no. 5 (2020): 676–92.
19. Akil Bello, 'How Test Publishers Are Poised to Profit From Pandemic "Learning Loss"', *Forbes*, 7 April 2021, https://www.forbes.com/sites/akilbello/2021/04/07/how-test-publishers-are-poised-to-profit-from-pandemic-learning-loss.
20. Dana Goldstein, 'Does It Hurt Children to Measure Pandemic Learning Loss?', *New York Times*, 8 April 2021, https://www.nytimes.com/2021/04/08/us/school-testing-education-covid.html.
21. Bello, 'How Test Publishers'.
22. Marx, *Capital, Vol. 1*.
23. Melamed, 'Racial Capitalism'.
24. Marx, *Capital, Vol. 1*, 355.
25. Karl Marx and Friedrich Engels, *The Communist Manifesto* [1848] (London: Vintage, 2010), 21.
26. Moreton-Robinson, *The White Possessive*.
27. Bruce Pascoe, *Dark Emu: Black Seeds Agriculture or Accident?* (Broome: Magabala Books, 2014).
28. Wolfe, 'Land, Labor, and Difference', 868.
29. Hage, *White Nation*; Lake and Reynolds, *Drawing the Global Colour Line*.

30. Jodi A. Byrd, Alyosha Goldstein, Jodi Melamed and Chandan Reddy, 'Predatory Value: Economies of Dispossession and Disturbed Relationalities', *Social Text* 36, no. 2 (2018): 9.
31. Byrd et al., 'Predatory Value', 3.
32. Sharon Stein, 'A Colonial History of the Higher Education Present: Rethinking Land-Grant Institutions through Processes of Accumulation and Relations of Conquest', *Critical Studies in Education* 61, no. 2 (2020): 212–28; for details, maps and narratives, see the database compiled by Robert Lee, Tristan Ahtone, Margaret Pearce, Kalen Goodluck, Geoff McGhee, Cody Leff, Katherine Lanpher and Taryn Salinas, 'Land Grab Universities', *High Country News*, https://www.landgrabu.org.
33. Moreton-Robinson, *The White Possessive*.
34. Julia Horne and Geoffrey Sherington, 'Extending the Educational Franchise: The Social Contract of Australia's Public Universities, 1850–1890', *Paedagogica Historica* 46, no. 1–2 (2010): 207–27; Gwilym Croucher and James Waghorne, *Australian Universities: A History of Common Cause* (Sydney: New South Publishing, 2020).
35. Nicolas Peterson, Lindy Allen and Louise Hamby, *The Makers and Making of Indigenous Australian Museum Collections* (Melbourne: Melbourne University Publishing, 2008); Victorian Aboriginal Heritage Council, 'Repatriation of Ceremonial Objects and Human Remains Under the UN Declaration on the Rights of Indigenous Peoples: Submission by the Victorian Aboriginal Heritage Council to the Expert Mechanism on the Rights of Indigenous People', 24 June 2020, https://www.aboriginalheritagecouncil.vic.gov.au/report-repatriation-ceremonial-objects-and-human-remains-under-un-declaration-rights-indigenous.
36. Natassia Chrysanthos, 'Inner West School to Spend Millions on Public Park Upgrade under Council Deal', *Sydney Morning Herald*, 7 May 2020, https://www.smh.com.au/national/nsw/inner-west-school-to-spend-millions-on-public-park-upgrade-under-council-deal-20200504-p54ppe.html.
37. ABC News (Australia), 'Government Unfurls School Flagpole Plan', 25 January 2005, https://www.abc.net.au/news/2005–01–25/government-unfurls-school-flagpole-plan/625004.

38. Commonwealth of Australia, 'National Framework for Values Education in Australian Schools', Department of Communications, Information Technology and the Arts, 2005, http://www.curriculum.edu.au/verve/_resources/Framework_PDF_version_for_the_web.pdf.
39. Moreton-Robinson, *The White Possessive*; see also Joshua Bennett, *Being Property Once Myself: Blackness and the End of Man* (Cambridge, MA: Harvard University Press, 2020).
40. Sanmati Verma, 'Kagaz Nahi Dikhayenge / We Won't Show Our Papers', *Peril Magazine*, 24 August 2020, no. 42, https://peril.com.au/back-editions/edition-42/we-wont-show-our-papers; Catherine Powell, 'The Color and Gender of COVID: Essential Workers, Not Disposable People', Think Global Health blog, 4 June 2020, https://www.thinkglobalhealth.org/article/color-and-gender-covid-essential-workers-not-disposable-people.
41. Raewyn Connell, Gary Dowsett and Sandra Kessler, *Making the Difference: Schools, Families and Social Division* (Sydney: George Allen & Unwin, 1982). See also Samuel Bowles and Herbert Gintis, *Schooling in Capitalist America: Educational Reform and the Contradictions of Economic Life* (New York: Basic Books, 1976); Paul E. Willis, *Learning to Labour: How Working Class Kids Get Working Class Jobs* (Farnborough: Saxon House, 1977); Jean Anyon, 'Social Class and the Hidden Curriculum of Work', *Journal of Education* 162 (1980): 67–92; Michael W. Apple, *Ideology and Curriculum* (London: Routledge & Kegan Paul, 1979).
42. Will Higginbotham, 'Blackbirding: Australia's History of Kidnapping Pacific Islanders', ABC News (Australia), 16 September 2017, https://www.abc.net.au/news/2017–09–17/blackbirding-australias-history-of-kidnapping-pacific-islanders/8860754.
43. Melissa Compagnoni, 'Servant or Slave: Reshaping Australian History through a New Lens', SBS/NITV Radio, 9 December 2016, https://www.sbs.com.au/language/english/servant-or-slave-reshaping-australian-history-through-a-new-lens.
44. See, for example Curthoys and Moore, 'Working for the White People'. The Queensland government has recently settled a stolen

wages case for AUS$190 million, recognising the unpaid labour of thousands of Indigenous people between 1939 and 1972.

45. Marilyn Lake, *Progressive New World: How Settler Colonialism and Transpacific Exchange Shaped American Reform* (Cambridge, MA: Harvard University Press, 2019).
46. Marilyn Lake, 'The White Man under Siege: New Histories of Race in the Nineteenth Century and the Advent of White Australia', *History Workshop Journal* 58, no. 1 (2004): 41–62.
47. Lisa Hall, '"Not Looking at Us Level": Systemic Barriers Faced by Aboriginal Teachers in Remote Communities in Central Australia', *Journal of Critical Race Inquiry* 5, no. 1 (2018): 74–101.
48. Hall, '"Not Looking at Us Level"'.
49. See, for example, Niranjan Robert Casinader and Lucas Walsh, 'Teacher Transculturalism and Cultural Difference: Addressing Racism in Australian Schools', *International Education Journal: Comparative Perspectives* 14, no. 2 (2015): 51–62.
50. Mayssoun Sukarieh and Stuart Tannock, 'Subcontracting Academia: Alienation, Exploitation and Disillusionment in the UK Overseas Syrian Refugee Research Industry', *Antipode* 51, no. 2 (2019): 664–80.
51. Sukarieh and Tannock, 'Subcontracting Academia', 666.
52. Jessica Gerrard and Rosie Barron, 'Cleaning Public Education: The Privatisation of School Maintenance Work', *Journal of Educational Administration and History* 52, no. 1 (2020): 9–21.
53. Leia Maia Donda, 'Why Won't UCL Treat Us Cleaners Like Its Other Staff?', *Guardian*, 4 December 2019, http://www.theguardian.com/commentisfree/2019/dec/04/ucl-cleaners-strike-outsourced-staff.
54. Cathy Free, 'Portraits on Campus Lacked Diversity, So This Artist Painted the Blue-Collar Workers Who "Really Run Things"', *Washington Post*, 24 January 2020, https://www.washingtonpost.com/lifestyle/2020/01/24/portraits-campus-lacked-diversity-so-this-artist-painted-blue-collar-workers-who-really-run-things.
55. United Workers Union, 'ACT School Cleaners Celebrate Success of "Backsourcing" Their Jobs', 12 February 2020, https://www.unitedworkers.org.au/act-school-cleaners-celebrate-success-of-backsourcing-their-jobs; see also Laurie Berg and Bassina

Farbenblum, *Wage Theft in Australia: Findings of the National Temporary Migrant Work Survey* (New South Wales: Migrant Worker Justice Initiative, 2017), https://www.mwji.org/survey; Gerrard and Barron, 'Cleaning Public Education'.

56. Tithi Bhattacharya, ed., *Social Reproduction Theory: Remapping Class, Recentering Oppression* (London: Pluto Press, 2017).
57. Lisa Marie Cacho, *Social Death: Racialized Rightlessness and the Criminalization of the Unprotected* (New York: New York University Press, 2012), 33.
58. Anthea Vogl and Elyse Methven, 'Life in the Shadow Carceral State: Surveillance and Control of Refugees in Australia', *International Journal for Crime, Justice and Social Democracy* 9, no. 4 (2020): 61–75; Thalia Anthony, '"They Were Treating Me Like a Dog": The Colonial Continuum of State Harms against Indigenous Children in Detention in the Northern Territory, Australia', *State Crime Journal* 7, no. 2 (2018): 251–77; Behrouz Boochani, *No Friend But the Mountains: Writing from Manus Prison* (Sydney: Pan Macmillan Australia, 2018).
59. We note here the emerging literature on the assetisation and financialisation of education which examines the interactions and operations of advanced capitalism and its technoscientific forms. See, for example, Kean Birch and Fabian Muniesa, *Assetization: Turning Things into Assets in Technoscientific Capitalism* (Cambridge, MA: MIT Press, 2020); Bob Jessop, 'Varieties of Academic Capitalism and Entrepreneurial Universities', *Higher Education* 73, no. 6 (2017): 853–70. Much of this literature has not to date examined how these relations of technoscientific capitalism are interlocked with racialisation and, as Tressie McMillan Cottom argues, there is a need for fuller understanding of the constitutive technologies of racism and capitalism in such analyses. See Tressie McMillan Cottom, 'Where Platform Capitalism and Racial Capitalism Meet: The Sociology of Race and Racism in the Digital Society', *Sociology of Race and Ethnicity* 6, no. 4 (2020): 441–9.
60. John Ross, 'Living Off the Land: The Universities Reaping the Rewards of Their Locations', *Times Higher Education*, 24 October 2019, https://www.timeshighereducation.com/features/living-land-universities-reaping-rewards-their-locations. In the US

context, Davarian Baldwin has recently examined the ways universities dispossess and extract from local communities through urban encroachment and expansion. Davarian L. Baldwin, *In the Shadow of the Ivory Tower: How Universities Are Plundering Our Cities* (New York: Bold Type Books, 2021).

61. Andrew Baldwin, 'Whiteness and Futurity: Towards a Research Agenda', *Progress in Human Geography* 36, no. 2 (2012): 172–87.
62. Christina Ho, 'My School and Others: Segregation and White Flight', *Australian Review of Public Affairs* 10, no. 1 (2011): 1–2.
63. David Golding and Kyle Kopsick, 'The Colonial Legacy in Cambridge Assessment Literature Syllabi', *Curriculum Perspectives* 39, no. 1 (2019): 7–17.
64. Queensland Government, 'Study at Queensland Offshore School', Department of Education International, trading as Education Queensland International, https://eqi.com.au/study-options/study-qld-offshore-school.
65. Francesca Martin, 'Chinese International Students' Wellbeing in Australia: The Road to Recovery', Report, University of Melbourne, 9 June 2020, http://minerva-access.unimelb.edu.au/handle/11343/240399.
66. On the dynamics of social exclusion and wage exploitation see Martin, 'Chinese International Students'. The resurgence of anti-Chinese racism in Australia and its impact on the international student 'market' is reported in Bill Birtles, 'China Cautions Students about "Racist Incidents" During Coronavirus Pandemic If They Return to Australia', ABC News (Australia), 9 June 2020, https://www.abc.net.au/news/2020-06-09/china-warns-students-not-to-return-to-australia-after-coronaviru/12337044.
67. Luke Henriques-Gomes, '"Callous Treatment": International Students Stranded in Australia Struggle to Survive', *Guardian*, 16 September 2020, http://www.theguardian.com/australia-news/2020/sep/17/callous-treatment-international-students-stranded-in-australia-struggle-to-survive. See also A.T. Le, 'Support for Doctoral Candidates in Australia During the Pandemic: The Case of the University of Melbourne', *Studies in Higher Education*, 46, no. 1 (2021): 133–45.

68. Leigh Patel, 'Desiring Diversity and Backlash: White Property Rights in Higher Education', *The Urban Review* 47, no. 4 (2015): 657–75.
69. Babalwa Magoqwana, Qawekazi Maqabuka and Malehoko Tshoaedi, '"Forced to Care" at the Neoliberal University: Invisible Labour as Academic Labour Performed by Black Women Academics in the South African University', *South African Review of Sociology* 50, no. 3–4 (2019): 6–21; Laura E. Hirshfield and Tiffany D. Joseph, '"We Need a Woman, We Need a Black Woman": Gender, Race, and Identity Taxation in the Academy', *Gender and Education* 24, no. 2 (2012): 213–27; Eric Anthony Grollman, 'Invisible Labor', *Inside Higher Ed*, 15 December 2015, https://www.insidehighered.com/advice/2015/12/15/column-about-exploitation-minority-scholars-academe.
70. Amy Thunig and Tiffany Jones, '"Don't Make Me Play House-N***er": Indigenous Academic Women Treated as "Black Performer" within Higher Education', *The Australian Educational Researcher* 48, no. 3 (1 July 2021): 397–417.
71. Kundnani, 'What is Racial Capitalism?'
72. Basil Bernstein, ed., *Class, Codes and Control, Vol. 2* (London: Routledge and Kegan Paul, 1973).
73. Saidiya V. Hartman, 'Saidiya Hartman on Insurgent Histories and the Abolitionist Imaginary', *Artforum*, 14 July 2020, https://www.artforum.com/interviews/saidiya-hartman-83579.
74. Cacho, *Social Death*, 33, original emphasis.

Chapter 4

1. Moreton-Robinson, *The White Possessive*, 131.
2. Anna Henderson, 'Prime Minister Tony Abbott Describes Sydney as "Nothing But Bush" Before First Fleet Arrived in 1788', ABC News (Australia), 14 November 2014, https://www.abc.net.au/news/2014–11–14/abbot-describes-1778-australia-as-nothing-but-bush/5892608.
3. James Norman, 'Why We Are Banning Tourists from Climbing Uluru', *The Conversation*, 6 November 2017, http://the

conversation.com/why-we-are-banning-tourists-from-climbing-uluru-86755.

4. Moreton-Robinson, *The White Possessive*, xiii.
5. Moreton-Robinson, *The White Possessive*, xi.
6. Frantz Fanon, *The Wretched of the Earth* [1961] (Harmondsworth: Penguin Books, 1969), 169.
7. Sabelo J. Ndlovu-Gatsheni, ed., *Epistemic Freedom in Africa: Deprovincialization and Decolonization* (London: Routledge, 2018), 3.
8. Finex Ndhlovu, 'Post-refugee African Australians' Perceptions about Being and Becoming Australian: Language, Discourse and Participation', *African Identities* 9, no. 4 (2011): 435–53.
9. Ndhlovu, 'Post-refugee African Australians', 450.
10. Boaventura de Sousa Santos, *Epistemologies of the South: Justice against Epistemicide* (Abingdon: Routledge, 2015).
11. Wolfe, 'Settler Colonialism and the Elimination of the Native'.
12. Commonwealth of Australia, *Bringing Them Home: Report of the National Inquiry into the Separation of Aboriginal and Torres Strait Islander Children from Their Families* (Sydney: Human Rights and Equal Opportunity Commission, 1997). See also Larissa Behrendt, 'Genocide: The Distance between Law and Life', *Aboriginal History* 25 (2001): 132–47. For an examination of education and genocide under Canadian settler colonialism, see Andrew Woolford and James Gacek, 'Genocidal Carcerality and Indian Residential Schools in Canada', *Punishment & Society* 18, no. 4 (2016): 400–19. At the time of writing, there are ongoing discoveries of the remains of hundreds of children at residential schools in Canada. See, for example, Tracey Lindeman, 'Canada: Remains of 215 Children Found at Indigenous Residential School Site', *Guardian*, 28 May 2021, http://www.theguardian.com/world/2021/may/28/canada-remains-indigenous-children-mass-graves.
13. Ndvolu-Gatenshi, *Epistemic Freedom*, 3.
14. De Sousa Santos, *Epistemologies of the South*.
15. Eve Tuck and Rubén A. Gaztambide-Fernández, 'Curriculum, Replacement, and Settler Futurity', *Journal of Curriculum Theorizing* 29, no. 1 (2013): 72–89.

16. This discussion of the hope and violence of education draws on our previous work: Sophie Rudolph, Arathi Sriprakash and Jessica Gerrard, 'Knowledge and Racial Violence: The Shine and Shadow of "Powerful Knowledge"', *Ethics and Education* 13, no. 1 (2018): 22–38.
17. Nakata, *Disciplining the Savages*, 276.
18. Nakata, *Disciplining the Savages*, 357.
19. Nakata, *Disciplining the Savages*, 314.
20. Matilda Keynes and Beth Marsden, 'Ontology, Sovereignty, Legitimacy: Two Key Moments When History Curriculum Was Challenged in Public Discourse and the Curricular Effects, Australia 1950s and 2000s', *History of Education Review* 50, no. 2 (2021): 130–45.
21. Daphne Martschenko, '"The Train Has Left the Station": The Arrival of the Biosocial Sciences in Education', *Research in Education* 107, no. 1 (2020): 3–9; Ben Williamson, 'Bringing Up the Bio-Datafied Child: Scientific and Ethical Controversies over Computational Biology in Education', *Ethics and Education* 15, no. 4 (2020): 444–63.
22. Ruha Benjamin, 'Catching Our Breath: Critical Race STS and the Carceral Imagination', *Engaging Science, Technology, and Society* 2 (2016): 145–56. The term 'delegated futures' is from Achille Mbembe, *Critique of Black Reason* (Durham, NC: Duke University Press, 2017).
23. Dorothy Roberts, 'The Ethics of Biosocial Science', The Tanner Lectures on Human Values, delivered at Harvard University, 2–3 November 2016.
24. David Gillborn, 'Softly, Softly: Genetics, Intelligence and the Hidden Racism of the New Geneism', *Journal of Education Policy* 31, no. 4 (2016): 365–88.
25. For an analysis of how eugenics and education have been historically entangled as part of the Australian project of settler colonialism, see Rob Watts, 'Beyond Nature and Nurture: Eugenics in Twentieth Century Australian History', *Australian Journal of Politics & History* 40, no. 3 (1994): 318–34. For a discussion of the emerging networks of psychodata that are forming pervasive metrics for education globally, see Ben Williamson, 'Psychodata:

Disassembling the Psychological, Economic, and Statistical Infrastructure of "Social-Emotional Learning"', *Journal of Education Policy* 36, no. 1 (2021): 129–54.

26. Sophie Rudolph, 'The Past in the Present: Identifying the Violence of Success and the Relief of Failure', in *The Relationality of Race in Education Research*, ed. Greg Vass, Jacinta Maxwell, Sophie Rudolph and Kalervo N. Gulson (London: Routledge, 2018), 145–55.
27. Maggie Walter, 'The Voice of Indigenous Data: Beyond the Markers of Disadvantage', *Griffith Review*, no. 60 (2018): 256–63.
28. Nakata, *Disciplining the Savages.*
29. Melitta Hogarth, 'The Power of Words: Bias and Assumptions in the Aboriginal and Torres Strait Islander Education Action Plan', *The Australian Journal of Indigenous Education* 46, no. 1 (2017): 44–53.
30. See also Tracey Bunda, Lew Zipin and Marie Brennan, 'Negotiating University "Equity" from Indigenous Standpoints: A Shaky Bridge', *International Journal of Inclusive Education* 16, no. 9 (2012): 941–57. The authors discuss how First Nations students are used 'to fill a gap within universities merely by being present, embodying cultural difference without significant change to the status quo' (941–2).
31. Sandra Taylor and Ravinder Kaur Sidhu, 'Supporting Refugee Students in Schools: What Constitutes Inclusive Education?', *International Journal of Inclusive Education* 16, no. 1 (2012): 39–56. See also Tebeje Molla, 'Refugees and Equity Policy in Australian Higher Education', *Policy Reviews in Higher Education* 5, no. 1 (2021): 5–27.
32. See, for example, Gurminder Bhambra, *Rethinking Modernity: Postcolonialism and the Sociological Imagination* (Basingstoke: Palgrave Macmillan, 2007); Bryan W. Van Norden, *Taking Back Philosophy* (New York: Columbia University Press, 2019); Raewyn Connell, *Southern Theory: The Global Dynamics of Knowledge in Social Science* (Cambridge: Polity, 2007).
33. Ian J. McNiven and Lynette Russell, *Appropriated Pasts: Indigenous Peoples and the Colonial Culture of Archaeology* (London: Rowman Altamira, 2005).

34. Michael Young and Johan Muller, 'On the Powers of Powerful Knowledge', *Review of Education* 1, no. 3 (2013): 229–50.
35. Some examples include the work of: Cargo Classroom, https://cargomovement.org/classroom; The Black Curriculum, https://theblackcurriculum.com; Learn Our Truth, https://learnourtruth.com.
36. Garma Festival's Youth Forum, 'The Imagination Declaration of the Youth Forum Read at Garma 2019', NITV, 5 August 2019, https://www.sbs.com.au/nitv/nitv-news/article/2019/08/05/imagination-declaration-youth-forum-read-garma-2019. The Uluru Statement from the Heart was a document created in 2017 following regional dialogues and a convention of First Nations people which discussed possibilities for constitutional change. It calls for First Nations voice in parliament, a commitment to truth telling and a treaty process. See The Uluru Statement, 'The Uluru Statement from the Heart', https://ulurustatement.org/the-statement.
37. Garma Festival's Youth Forum, 'The Imagination Declaration'.
38. Learn our Truth, 'Why Are We Not Learning Our Truth?', https://learnourtruth.com/about/#faqs.
39. Learn our Truth, 'Educator Pledge', https://learnourtruth.com/educator-pledge.
40. See Megan Davis, 'The Long Road to Uluru: Walking Together: Truth before Justice', *Griffith Review*, no. 60 (2018); Harry Hobbs, 'Victoria's Truth-telling Commission: To Move Forward, We Need to Answer For the Legacies of Colonisation', *The Conversation*, 9 March 2021, http://theconversation.com/victorias-truth-telling-commission-to-move-forward-we-need-to-answer-for-the-legacies-of-colonisation-156746.
41. Walter Mignolo, *Local Histories/Global Designs: Coloniality, Subaltern Knowledges, and Border Thinking* (Princeton: Princeton University Press, 2000), 22.
42. Cash Ahenakew, Vanessa De Oliveira Andreotti, Garrick Cooper and Hemi Hireme, 'Beyond Epistemic Provincialism: De-Provincializing Indigenous Resistance', *AlterNative: An International Journal of Indigenous Peoples* 10, no. 3 (2014): 219.

43. Charles W. Mills, *Black Rights/White Wrongs: The Critique of Racial Liberalism* (Oxford: Oxford University Press, 2017).
44. Mills, 'White Ignorance'.
45. The production and strategic use of ignorance in social and political life has been the subject of the growing field of ignorance studies. See, for example, Matthias Gross and Linsey McGoey, *Routledge International Handbook of Ignorance Studies* (London: Routledge, 2015); and, with a focus on race, Sullivan and Tuana's edited volume, *Race and Epistemologies of Ignorance*.
46. Charles W. Mills, 'Global White Ignorance', in *Routledge International Handbook of Ignorance Studies*, ed. Gross and McGoey, 217.
47. Bernard Smith, *The Spectre of Truganini* (Sydney: Australian Broadcasting Commission, 1980), 22. See also Bain Attwood, 'Denial in a Settler Society: The Australian Case', *History Workshop Journal* 84 (1 October 2017): 24–43.
48. As Charles W. Mills also explores, the social contract is, in fact, a racial contract, as its terms and norms underwrite the political system of white supremacy. Charles W. Mills, *Racial Contract* (Ithaca: Cornell University Press, 1999).
49. Penny Skye Taylor and Daphne Habibis, 'Widening the Gap: White Ignorance, Race Relations and the Consequences for Aboriginal People in Australia', *Australian Journal of Social Issues* 55, no. 3 (2020): 354–71.
50. Sabelo J. Ndlovu-Gatsheni, '"Moral Evil, Economic Good": Whitewashing the Sins of Colonialism', Al Jazeera, 26 February 2021, https://www.aljazeera.com/opinions/2021/2/26/colonialism-in-africa-empire-was-not-ethical.
51. For analyses of how liberal prescriptions on progress and freedom emerge from and are implicated in imperial expansionism and racial hierarchies, see Uday Singh Mehta, *Liberalism and Empire: A Study in Nineteenth-Century British Liberal Thought* (Chicago: University of Chicago Press, 2018).
52. Mills, 'Global White Ignorance', 219.
53. Mills, 'White ignorance', 31. Also see discussions of the freezing of racism in historical time in Alana Lentin, 'Racism in Public or

Public Racism: Doing Anti-racism in "Post-Racial" Times', *Ethnic and Racial Studies* 39, no. 1 (2016): 33–48.

54. Mills, 'White ignorance', 29.
55. Zara Bain, 'Is There Such a Thing as "White Ignorance" in British Education?', *Ethics and Education* 13, no. 1 (2 January 2018): 12.
56. Over 40,000 people marched in Sydney to protest the bicentenary celebrations, the largest march to have occurred in the city at the time. See Deadly Story, 'The 1988 Bicentenary Protest', https://www.deadlystory.com/page/culture/history/The_1988_Bicentenary_Protest.
57. Robyn Moore's recent analysis of secondary textbooks offers another example of how education produces and maintains representations of Australia as a white nation. She argues that school textbooks are complicit in 'representing events from a White perspective, privileging White interests, and by focusing disproportionately on Whites' (70). Robyn Moore, 'Who Is Australian? National Belonging and Exclusion in Australian History Textbooks', *Review of Education* 9, no. 1 (2021): 55–77.
58. For an analysis of historical erasures in higher education, through the experiences of First Nations and transcultural doctoral students, see Jing Qi, Catherine Manathunga, Michael Singh and Tracey Bunda, 'Transcultural and First Nations Doctoral Education and Epistemological Border-Crossing: Histories and Epistemic Justice', *Teaching in Higher Education* 26, no. 3 (3 April 2021): 340–53.
59. Peta Salter and Jacinta Maxwell, 'The Inherent Vulnerability of the Australian Curriculum's Cross-Curriculum Priorities', *Critical Studies in Education* 57, no. 3 (2016): 296–312.
60. Tony Taylor, 'Pyne Curriculum Review Prefers Analysis-free Myth to History', *The Conversation*, 20 October 2014, http://theconversation.com/pyne-curriculum-review-prefers-analysis-free-myth-to-history-32956.
61. Kevin Donnelly, *How Political Correctness Is Destroying Australia: Enemies within and Without* (Melbourne: Wilkinson Publishing, 2018).
62. Stewart Riddle, 'Australian Curriculum Review: Strengthened But Still a Long Way from an Amazing Curriculum for All Australian

Students', *EduResearch Matters*, 3 May 2021, https://www.aare.edu.au/blog/?p=9311.

63. Triple J Hack, 'Education Minister Tells Hack Proposed School History Curriculum is "Overly Negative" and "Downplaying Western Civilisation"', ABC (Australia), 8 September 2021, https://www.abc.net.au/triplej/programs/hack/education-minister-tells-hack-proposed-school-history-curriculu/13532152.
64. Nick Riemer, 'Weaponising Learning', *Sydney Review of Books*, 12 June 2018, https://sydneyreviewofbooks.com/essay/weaponising-learning.
65. Tony Abbott, 'Paul Ramsay's Vision for Australia', *Quadrant Online*, 24 May 2018, https://quadrant.org.au/magazine/2018/04/paul-ramsays-vision-australia.
66. Ramsay Health Care, 'Former Prime Ministers Launch Ramsay Centre for Western Civilisation', 8 January 2018, https://www.ramsayhealth.com/News/General-News/Former-Prime-Ministers-launch-Ramsay-Centre-for-Western-Civilisation.
67. Daniel Trilling, 'Why Is the UK Government Suddenly Targeting "Critical Race Theory"?', *Guardian*, 23 October 2020, http://www.theguardian.com/commentisfree/2020/oct/23/uk-critical-race-theory-trump-conservatives-structural-inequality. See also Bain's discussions of how white ignorance in the UK 'fights back'. Bain, 'Is There Such a Thing', 12.
68. Wade Zaglas, 'IPA Program Director Takes Aim at Anti-racism Program', *Education Review*, 8 April 2021, https://www.educationreview.com.au/2021/04/worse-than-safe-schools-ipa-program-director-takes-aim-at-anti-racism-website.
69. Bella d'Abrera, 'University Audit Finds Humanities Riddled With Critical Race Theory and Identity Politics', Institute of Public Affairs, 16 January 2021, https://ipa.org.au/ipa-today/university-audit-finds-humanities-riddled-with-critical-race-theory-and-identity-politics.
70. Michael Safi, 'New Extremism Guidelines Require Schools to Report Suspect Behaviour', *Guardian*, 4 March 2016, http://www.theguardian.com/australia-news/2016/mar/04/new-extremism-guidelines-require-schools-to-report-suspect-behaviour. See also Shahram Akbarzadeh, 'Investing in Mentoring and Educational

Initiatives: The Limits of De-Radicalisation Programmes in Australia', *Journal of Muslim Minority Affairs* 33, no. 4 (1 December 2013): 451–63.

71. Jessica Gerrard, 'Whose Public, Which Public? The Challenge for Public Education', *Critical Studies in Education* 59, no. 2 (2018): 211.
72. Emma Rowe, 'Reading Islamophobia in Education Policy through a Lens of Critical Race Theory: A Study of the "Funding Freeze" for Private Islamic Schools in Australia', *Whiteness and Education* 5, no. 1 (2020): 54–73.
73. Helen Proctor and Arathi Sriprakash, 'Race and Legitimacy: Historical Formations of Academically Selective Schooling in Australia', *Journal of Ethnic and Migration Studies* 43, no. 14 (2017): 2378–92.
74. Mills, 'Global White Ignorance', 218.
75. Alison Holland, 'Black Lives Matter Has Brought a Global Reckoning with History. This Is Why the Uluru Statement Is So Crucial', *The Conversation*, 21 December 2020, https://theconversation.com/black-lives-matter-has-brought-a-global-reckoning-with-history-this-is-why-the-uluru-statement-is-so-crucial-149974.
76. Lewis Williams, Tracey Bunda, Nick Claxton and Iain MacKinnon, 'A Global De-Colonial Praxis of Sustainability – Undoing Epistemic Violences between Indigenous Peoples and Those No Longer Indigenous to Place', *The Australian Journal of Indigenous Education* 47, no. 1 (2018): 41–53.

Chapter 5

1. Sara Ahmed, 'Affective Economies', *Social Text* 22, no. 2 (2004): 117–39.
2. Jane Kenway and Johannah Fahey, 'Public Pedagogies and Global Emoscapes', *Pedagogies: An International Journal* 6, no. 2 (2011): 169.
3. Sara Ahmed, 'The Politics of Bad Feeling', *Australasian Journal of Critical Race and Whiteness Studies* 1 (2005): 72.
4. Kenway and Fahey, 'Public Pedagogies', 169.

5. Megan Boler, *Feeling Power: Emotions and Education* (London: Routledge, 1999), xvii.
6. Bain Attwood, 'Denial in a Settler Society: The Australian Case', *History Workshop Journal* 84 (1 October 2017): 24–43.
7. See, for example, Charles W. Mills, 'White Time: The Chronic Injustice of Ideal Theory 1', *Du Bois Review* 11, no. 1 (2014): 27–42.
8. Moreton-Robinson, *The White Possessive*, 20.
9. Moreton-Robinson, *The White Possessive*, 20.
10. Peter Cochrane, *Best We Forget: The War for White Australia, 1914–18* (Melbourne: Text Publishing, 2018).
11. Eva Mackey, *Unsettled Expectations: Uncertainty, Land and Settler Decolonization* (Halifax & Winnipeg: Fernwood Publishing, 2016), 70–100.
12. Mackey, *Unsettled Expectations*, 35.
13. Mackey, *Unsettled Expectations*, 70–100.
14. Lisa Slater, *Anxieties of Belonging in Settler Colonialism: Australia, Race and Place* (London: Routledge, 2019).
15. Helen Ngo, *The Habits of Racism: A Phenomenology of Racism and Racialized Embodiment* (Lanham: Lexington Books, 2017), 97–101.
16. For a discussion of the notion of home in settler colonialism see also Tuck and Yang, 'Decolonization Is Not a Metaphor'; Tuck and Gaztambide-Fernández, 'Curriculum, Replacement, and Settler Futurity'.
17. Ngo, *The Habits of Racism*, 101.
18. Marilyn Lake, Henry Reynolds, Mark McKenna and Joy Damousi, *What's Wrong with ANZAC? The Militarisation of Australian History* (Sydney: University of NSW Press, 2010), 3.
19. Conor Duffy, '"Brandzac Day": Historian Criticises "New Low in the Commercialisation of Anzac"', ABC News (Australia), 15 April 2015, https://www.abc.net.au/news/2015-04-15/critics-disgusted-by-vulgar-commercialisation-of-anzac-day/6395756.
20. Marilyn Lake, 'How Do Schoolchildren Learn about the Spirit of Anzac?', in *What's Wrong with ANZAC?*, ed. Lake et al, 135–56.
21. Lake et al., *What's Wrong with ANZAC?*, 1.
22. Lake et al., *What's Wrong with ANZAC?*, 1.

23. ABC News (Australia), 'Yassmin Abdel-Magied: ABC Can't Sweep Presenter's Anzac Day Controversy under the Carpet, Joyce Says', 26 April 2017, https://www.abc.net.au/news/2017-04-26/yassmin-abdel-magied-under-fire-for-anzac-post/8472414.
24. ABC, 'Yassmin Abdel-Magied'. A similar situation occurred a couple of years earlier when a white employee of public broadcaster SBS tweeted comments that were considered inflammatory, but in fact acknowledged the suffering and complexity of war and violence from multiple perspectives as well as the arrogance of whiteness. See Louise Hall, 'Scott McIntyre Not Sacked for Controversial Anzac Day Opinion: SBS', *Sydney Morning Herald*, 17 December 2015, https://www.smh.com.au/business/companies/scott-mcintyre-not-sacked-for-controversial-anzac-day-opinion-sbs-20151217-glpwkt.html.
25. Richard Ackland, 'The Yassmin Abdel-Magied Bash-a-thon Is All Part of the Anzac Day Ritual', *Guardian*, 28 April 2017, http://www.theguardian.com/commentisfree/2017/apr/28/the-yassmin-abdel-magied-bash-a-thon-is-all-part-of-the-anzac-day-ritual.
26. Kathy Marks, 'The Anzac Post, Outrage and a Debate about Race', BBC News, 10 August 2017, https://www.bbc.com/news/world-australia-40712832.
27. See, for example, Jane Gilmore, 'Hysteria over Yassmin Abdel-Magied's Anzac Day Post Cannot Be Separated from Racism', *Sydney Morning Herald*, 27 April 2017 (updated 28 April 2017), https://www.smh.com.au/lifestyle/hysteria-over-yassmin-abdelmagieds-anzac-day-post-cannot-be-separated-from-racism-20170427-gvtjdj.html; Marks, 'The Anzac Post'. ANZAC day has also been critiqued for silencing the Frontier Wars during which Aboriginal people defended their land against colonial invasion; see Matt Chun, 'Enduring Silence: Anzac Day and the Frontier Wars', *Overland Literary Journal*, 3 May 2018, https://overland.org.au/2018/05/enduring-silence-anzac-day-and-the-frontier-wars.
28. Stein, 'Navigating Different Theories of Change'; see also Sharon Stein, Dallas Hunt, Rene Suša and Vanessa de Oliveira Andreotti, 'The Educational Challenge of Unraveling the Fantasies of

Ontological Security', *Diaspora, Indigenous, and Minority Education* 11, no. 2 (3 April 2017): 69–79.

29. Stein, 'Navigating Different Theories of Change', 15.
30. Stefano Gulmanelli, 'John Howard and the 'Anglospherist' Reshaping of Australia', *Australian Journal of Political Science* 49, no. 4 (2014): 581–95.
31. See John Chesterman and Brian Galligan, *Citizens without Rights: Aborigines and Australian Citizenship* (Cambridge: Cambridge University Press, 1997), 16.
32. Rosalind Kidd, *The Way We Civilise: Aboriginal Affairs – the Untold Story* (St Lucia: University of Queensland Press, 1997); see also a project on the history of Aboriginal exemption policies, Aboriginal Exemption website, https://aboriginalexemption.com.au.
33. Commonwealth of Australia, *Bringing Them Home: Report of the National Inquiry into the Separation of Aboriginal and Torres Strait Islander Children from Their Families*.
34. Jane Carey, '"Wanted! A Real White Australia": The Women's Movement, Whiteness and the Settler Colonial Project, 1900–1940', in *Studies in Settler Colonialism*, ed. Fiona Bateman and Lionel Pilkington (London: Springer, 2011), 122–39.
35. See ABC News (Australia), 'Aboriginal Children in Care "a New Stolen Generation", UTS Indigenous Researcher Says', 26 May 2014, https://www.abc.net.au/news/2014-05-26/stolen-generation-with-aboriginal-children-in-care-nt/5478898; Calla Wahlquist, 'Indigenous Children in Care Doubled since Stolen Generations Apology', *Guardian*, 25 January 2018, http://www.theguardian.com/australia-news/2018/jan/25/indigenous-children-in-care-doubled-since-stolen-generations-apology.
36. For example, in 2018 a popular current affairs TV programme, *Sunrise*, aired a discussion about Aboriginal child removal that involved an all-white panel and acted to bolster the image of the white 'saviour'. See the response by Darumbul journalist Amy McQuire, '"Saving the Children" Are the Three Most Dangerous Words Uttered By White People', *Guardian*, 14 March 2018, https://www.theguardian.com/commentisfree/2018/mar/14/saving-the-children-are-the-three-most-dangerous-words-uttered-by-white-people.

37. Sophie Rudolph and Lilly Brown, 'Understanding the Techniques of Colonialism: Indigenous Educational Justice', in *Powers of Curriculum: Sociological Perspectives on Education*, ed. Brad Gobby and Rebecca Walker (South Melbourne: Oxford University Press, 2017), 288–320; Bain Attwood and Andrew Markus, *The Struggle for Aboriginal Rights: A Documentary History* (St Leonards: Allen & Unwin, 1999).
38. See Mark Thomas, 'Your Country Needs You: BBQ Like You've Never BBQ'd Before This Australia Day' (Picture), https://catalogue.nla.gov.au/Record/4808652?lookfor=author:%22George%20Patterson%20Y%20&%20R%22&offset=1&max=3.
39. Mark Thomas, 'Australians Man Your Eskys This January 26' (Picture), https://catalogue.nla.gov.au/Record/4808857?lookfor=author:%22George%20Patterson%20Y%20&%20R%22&offset=3&max=3.
40. See Blagg and Anthony, '"Stone Walls Do Not a Prison Make"'; Andrea Smith, 'Indigeneity, Settler Colonialism, White Supremacy', in *Racial Formation in the Twenty-First Century*, ed. Daniel Martinez HoSang, Oneka LaBennett and Laura Puildo (Berkeley: University of California Press, 2012); Encarnación Gutiérrez Rodríguez, 'The Coloniality of Migration and the "Refugee Crisis": On the Asylum–Migration Nexus, the Transatlantic White European Settler Colonialism–Migration and Racial Capitalism', *Refuge: Canada's Journal on Refugees*, 34, no. 1 (2018): 16–28.
41. Ahmed, 'Multiculturalism and the Promise of Happiness'.
42. Ngo, *The Habits of Racism*, 107.
43. See Sara Ahmed, *On Being Included: Racism and Diversity in Institutional Life* (Durham, NC: Duke University Press, 2012). Ghassan Hage also discusses how domestication has been central to maintaining whiteness in the Australian settler colony. Domestication refers to 'a mode of inhabiting the world through dominating it for the purpose of making it yield value: material or symbolic forms of sustenance, comfort, aesthetic pleasure, and so on'. Hage, *Is Racism an Environmental Threat?*, 87.
44. See Jennifer Clark, *Aborigines & Activism: Race, Aborigines & the Coming of the Sixties to Australia* (Crawley: University of Western

Australia Press, 2008); Gary Foley, *A Short History of the Australian Indigenous Resistance 1950–1990* (Vancouver: Subversion Press, 2010); Fazal Rizvi, 'Multiculturalism in Australia: The Construction and Promotion of an Ideology', *Journal of Education Policy* 3, no. 4 (1988): 335–50.

45. Rizvi, 'Multiculturalism in Australia'.
46. See Sara Ahmed, 'The Language of Diversity', *Ethnic and Racial Studies* 30, no. 2 (2007): 235–56; Ghassan Hage, *Writings on Nationalism, Multiculturalism and Racism: Including White Nation and against Paranoid Nationalism* (Ultimo: Australian Society of Authors, 2014). See also Sophie Rudolph, *Unsettling the Gap: Race, Politics and Indigenous Education* (New York: Peter Lang, 2019).
47. John Howard, 'John Howard on Multiculturalism', transcript of address by The Prime Minister The Hon John Howard MP, Launch of the National Multicultural Advisory Council's Issues paper *Multicultural Australia: The Way Forward*, Melbourne Town Hall, 11 December 1997, http://www.multiculturalaustralia.gov.au/doc/howard_2.pdf. See also John William Tate, 'John Howard's "Nation": Multiculturalism, Citizenship, and Identity', *Australian Journal of Politics & History* 55, no. 1 (2009): 97–120.
48. Osmond Chiu, 'Eliminating Racism: Or As We Call It, Harmony', *Meanjin*, 20 March 2019, https://meanjin.com.au/blog/eliminating-racism-or-as-we-call-it-harmony.
49. Emma Rowe, *Middle-Class School Choice in Urban Spaces: The Economics of Public Schooling and Globalized Education Reform* (Abingdon: Routledge, 2017).
50. Timna Jacks, 'White Flight: Race Segregation in Melbourne State Schools', *The Age*, 2 May 2016, https://www.theage.com.au/national/victoria/white-flight-race-segregation-in-melbourne-state-schools-20160501-goj516.html.
51. Ien Ang, 'From White Australia to Fortress Australia: The Anxious Nation in the New Century', in *Legacies of White Australia: Race, Culture and Nation*, ed. L. Jayasuriya, D. Walker and J. Gothard (Perth: University of Western Australia Press, 2003), 51–70.
52. Brianne Tolj, 'Aboriginal Activist Calling For Australia to Be "Burnt to the Ground" Slammed as a "Hypocrite" Because She's Paid by Taxpayers', *Mail Online*, 29 January 2018, http://www.

dailymail.co.uk/news/article-5323383/Aboriginal-activist-said-Australia-burn-slammed.html. See also, Melissa Carey and Adam Cunningham, '"Invasion Day" Rally Organiser Says Her Comments Australia Should "Burn to the Ground" Should Not Be Taken Literally', *The Age*, 26 January 2018, https://www.theage.com.au/national/victoria/invasion-day-rally-organiser-says-her-comments-australia-should-burn-to-the-ground-should-not-be-taken-literally-20180126-p4yyxo.html.

53. Yu Ouyang, 'Australian Invention of Chinese Invasion: A Century of Paranoia, 1888/1988', *Australian Literary Studies* 17, no. 1 (1995): 74–83.
54. Anne Aly and David Walker, 'Veiled Threats: Recurrent Cultural Anxieties in Australia', *Journal of Muslim Minority Affairs* 27, no. 2 (1 August 2007): 203; for historical insights into the presence of Muslim people, knowledges and industries in the early settler colony, see Samia Khatun, *Australianama: The South Asian Odyssey in Australia* (Oxford: Oxford University Press, 2018).
55. Scott Poynting and Victoria Mason, 'The Resistible Rise of Islamophobia: Anti-Muslim Racism in the UK and Australia Before 11 September 2001', *Journal of Sociology* 43, no. 1 (2007): 61–86.
56. Shakira Hussein, Scheherazade Bloul and Scott Poynting, 'Diasporas and Dystopias on the Beach: Burkini Wars in France and Australia', in *Islamophobia and the Muslim Student: Disciplining the Intellect*, ed. Irene Zempi and Imran Awan (Abingdon: Routledge, 2019), 263–74.
57. We remember here that Australian Brenton Tarrant, the white supremacist terrorist who killed 51 people in 2019 at the Al Noor Mosque in Christchurch, New Zealand, grew up with these pedagogic messages.
58. Hage, *Is Racism an Environmental Threat?*, 9.
59. See Stella Coram and Chris Hallinan, 'Critical Race Theory and the Orthodoxy of Race Neutrality: Examining the Denigration of Adam Goodes', *Australian Aboriginal Studies*, no. 1 (2017); Ariadna Matamoros-Fernández, 'Platformed Racism: The Mediation and Circulation of an Australian Race-Based Controversy on Twitter, Facebook and YouTube', *Information, Communication & Society* 20, no. 6 (2017): 930–46.

60. For example, Blagg and Anthony, '"Stone Walls Do Not a Prison Make"'. See also Australian Law Reform Commission, 'Disproportionate Incarceration Rate', 9 January 2018, https://www.alrc.gov.au/publication/pathways-to-justice-inquiry-into-the-incarceration-rate-of-aboriginal-and-torres-strait-islander-peoples-alrc-report-133/executive-summary-15/disproportionate-incarceration-rate; Sentencing Advisory Council, 'Indigenous Young People in Detention', https://plotly.com/~SAC/375.
61. Paul Hodge, 'A Grievable Life? The Criminalisation and Securing of Asylum Seeker Bodies in the "Violent Frames" of Australia's Operation Sovereign Borders', *Geoforum* 58 (2015): 122–31.
62. See for example, John Gardiner, David Evans and Kenneth Howell, 'Suspension and Exclusion Rates for Aboriginal Students in Western Australia', *Aboriginal Child at School* 23, no. 1 (1995): 32; Sophie Rudolph, 'Ngaga-Dji, a Call to Action: Education Justice and Youth Imprisonment', *The Australian Educational Researcher* 48, no. 3 (1 July 2021): 433–48; Linda J. Graham, Tony McCarthy, Callula Killingly, Haley Tancredi and Shiralee Poed, 'Inquiry into Suspension, Exclusion and Expulsion Processes in South Australian Government Schools: Final Report', Brisbane: The Centre for Inclusive Education, QUT, 2020. Ombudsman's reports in Victoria and NSW in 2017 also refer to suspensions and expulsions and indicate that Aboriginal and Torres Strait Islander students are more likely to be suspended and expelled. See Victorian Ombudsman, 'Investigation into Victorian Government School Expulsion', 14 August 2017, https://www.ombudsman.vic.gov.au/our-impact/investigation-reports/investigation-into-victorian-government-school-expulsions; Ombudsman New South Wales, 'NSW Ombudsman Inquiry into Behaviour Management in Schools: A Special Report to Parliament under s 31 of the Ombudsman Act 1974', 9 August 2017, https://www.ombo.nsw.gov.au/news-and-publications/publications/reports/community-and-disability-services/nsw-ombudsman-inquiry-into-behaviour-management-in-schools-august-2017.
63. Eve Mayes, 'Radical Reform and Reforming Radicals in Australian Schooling', *History of Education Review* 48, no. 2 (2019): 156–70.

64. Shahram Akbarzadeh, 'Investing in Mentoring and Educational Initiatives: The Limits of De-Radicalisation Programmes in Australia', *Journal of Muslim Minority Affairs* 33, no. 4 (2013): 461. Akbarzadeh demonstrates how the marginalisation experienced is often material as well as psychological, with Muslim Australians being 2.5 times more likely than white Australians to be unemployed between 2006 and 2011.
65. Talissa Siganto, '9 yo Refuses to Stand Because Anthem Is For "White People of Australia"', ABC News (Australia), 12 September 2018, https://www.abc.net.au/news/2018-09-12/national-anthem-protest-school-brisbane/10235792.
66. Jessica Walton, Naomi Priest, Emma Kowal, Fiona White, Brandi Fox and Yin Paradies, 'Whiteness and National Identity: Teacher Discourses in Australian Primary Schools', *Race Ethnicity and Education* 21, no. 1 (2018): 132–47.
67. Jonnell Uptin, '"If I Peel Off My Black Skin Maybe Then I Integrate": Examining How African-Australian Youth Find Living in a "Post Multicultural" Australia', *Social Identities* 27, no. 1 (2021): 75–91.
68. Uptin, '"If I Peel"', 84.
69. Uptin, '"If I Peel"', 84.
70. Yukari Takimoto Amos, 'Voices of Teacher Candidates of Color on White Race Evasion: "I Worried about My Safety!"', *International Journal of Qualitative Studies in Education* 29, no. 8 (2016): 1003.
71. Bree Picower, 'The Unexamined Whiteness of Teaching: How White Teachers Maintain and Enact Dominant Racial Ideologies', *Race Ethnicity and Education* 12, no. 2 (2009): 197–215.
72. Picower, 'Unexamined Whiteness'.
73. Ahmed, 'The Politics of Bad Feeling'.
74. Ahmed, 'The Politics of Bad Feeling'; Ngo, *The Habits of Racism*.

Chapter 6

1. Teela Reid, '2020: The Year of Reckoning, Not Reconciliation. It's Time to Show Up', *Griffith Review* 67: Matters of Trust (2020), https://www.griffithreview.com/articles/2020-year-of-reckoning.

2. Sarah Maddison, Tom Clark and Ravi De Costa, *The Limits of Settler Colonial Reconciliation* (New York: Springer, 2016).
3. Paul Gilroy, *Postcolonial Melancholia* (New York: Columbia University Press, 2005), 56.
4. Charles W. Mills, *Black Rights/White Wrongs: The Critique of Racial Liberalism* (Oxford: Oxford University Press, 2017).
5. Alexis Shotwell, *Against Purity: Living Ethically in Compromised Times* (Minneapolis: University of Minnesota Press, 2016). On settler narcissism see Paul Muldoon, 'A Reconciliation Most Desirable: Shame, Narcissism, Justice and Apology', *International Political Science Review* 38, no. 2 (2017): 213–26. See also Sarah Maddison, *Beyond White Guilt: The Real Challenge of Black–White Relations in Australia* (Sydney: Allen & Unwin, 2011).
6. Aziz Choudry, *Learning Activism: The Intellectual Life of Contemporary Social Movements* (Toronto: University of Toronto Press, 2015), 12.
7. Irene Watson, 'Aboriginal Sovereignties: Past, Present and Future (Im)Possibilities', in *Our Patch: Enacting Australian Sovereignty Post-2001*, ed. Suvendrini Perera (Perth: API Network, 2007), 25.
8. Watson, 'Aboriginal Sovereignties', 28.
9. Ambelin Kwaymullina, *Living on Stolen Land* (Broome: Magabala Books, 2020), 64.
10. Kwaymullina, *Living on Stolen Land*, 58.
11. Keri Facer, 'Futures in Education: Towards an Ethical Practice', paper commissioned for the UNESCO Futures of Education report (2021), 3.
12. Facer, 'Futures in Education', 21–2.
13. Facer's analysis helpfully delineates different orientations between education and the future, including for example: education *in* the future which foregrounds predictive and imaginative orientations, and education *about* the future which foregrounds pedagogic and reflexive modes.
14. Facer, 'Futures in Education', 8.
15. Facer, 'Futures in Education', 10.
16. See also Ziauddin Sardar, 'Colonizing the Future: The "Other" Dimension of Futures Studies', *Futures* 25, no. 2 (1993): 179–87.

17. Andrew Baldwin, 'Whiteness and Futurity: Towards a Research Agenda', *Progress in Human Geography* 36, no. 2 (2012): 178.
18. Of course, this is not a political project that has operated with totalising success; enduring transnational movements and creative insurrections for Indigenous futurism, Afrofuturism and decolonial futures, among others, exist as testament to this. See for example Centre for Indigenous Global Futures, Macquarie University, https://www.mq.edu.au/research/research-centres-groups-and-facilities/resilient-societies/centres/forum-for-indigenous-research-excellence; Initiative for Indigenous Futures, http://indigenousfutures.net; Gesturing Towards Decolonial Futures, https://decolonialfutures.net; Grace Gipson, 'Creating and Imagining Black Futures through Afrofuturism', in *#identity: Hashtagging Race, Gender, Sexuality, and Nation*, ed. Abigail De Kosnik and Keith Feldman (Ann Arbor: University of Michigan Press, 2019), 84–103.
19. Facer, 'Futures in Education', 16. On the idea of hospicing unjust systems, see Sharon Stein, Vanessa Andreotti, Rene Suša, Sarah Amsler, Dallas Hunt, Cash Ahenakew, Elwood Jimmy, Tereza Cajkova, Will Valley and Camilla Cardoso, 'Gesturing towards Decolonial Futures: Reflections on Our Learnings Thus Far', *Nordic Journal of Comparative and International Education (NJCIE)* 4, no. 1 (2020): 43–65.
20. Facer, 'Futures in Education', 2.
21. Arathi Sriprakash, David Nally, Kevin Myers and Pedro Ramos Pinto, 'Learning with the Past: Racism, Education and Reparative Futures', paper commissioned for the UNESCO Futures of Education report (2020), 2.
22. Mills, 'White Time'.
23. Sonali Thakkar, 'Reparative Remembering', *WSQ: Women's Studies Quarterly* 48, no. 1 (2020): 137–40.
24. See for example Alexandra Alvaro, 'University of Tasmania's New Subject Aims to "Indigenise" Teaching', ABC News (Australia), 30 May 2021, https://www.abc.net.au/news/2021–05–31/tas-mon-utas-indigenous-learning-on-country/100176826; Jan Hare, Christine Bridge and Amber Shilling, 'Preparing Teachers through Land Education: Indigenous Erasure, Reclamation, and Resurgence

in Campus Spaces', in *Indigenous Futures and Learnings Taking Place*, ed. Ligia (Licho) López López and Gioconda Coello (London: Routledge, 2020), 138–56.

25. Joan Wallach Scott, *In the Name of History* (Budapest: Central European University Press, 2019).

Bibliography

Abbott, Tony. 'Paul Ramsay's Vision for Australia'. *Quadrant Online*, 24 May 2018. https://quadrant.org.au/magazine/2018/04/paul-ramsays-vision-australia.

ABC News (Australia). 'Aboriginal Children in Care "a New Stolen Generation", UTS Indigenous researcher says'. 26 May 2014. https://www.abc.net.au/news/2014–05–26/stolen-generation-with-aboriginal-children-in-care-nt/5478898.

ABC News (Australia). 'Government Unfurls School Flagpole Plan'. 25 January 2005. https://www.abc.net.au/news/2005–01–25/government-unfurls-school-flagpole-plan/625004.

ABC News (Australia). 'Yassmin Abdel-Magied: ABC Can't Sweep Presenter's Anzac Day Controversy under the Carpet, Joyce Says'. 26 April 2017. https://www.abc.net.au/news/2017–04–26/yassmin-abdel-magied-under-fire-for-anzac-post/8472414.

Abdel-Fattah, Randa. *Coming of Age in the War on Terror*. Sydney: New South Publishing, 2021.

Aboriginal Exemption website. https://aboriginalexemption.com.au.

Ackland, Richard. 'The Yassmin Abdel-Magied Bash-a-thon Is All Part of the Anzac Day Ritual'. *Guardian*, 28 April 2017. http://www.theguardian.com/commentisfree/2017/apr/28/the-yassmin-abdel-magied-bash-a-thon-is-all-part-of-the-anzac-day-ritual.

Ahenakew, Cash, Vanessa De Oliveira Andreotti, Garrick Cooper and Hemi Hireme. 'Beyond Epistemic Provincialism: De-Provincializing Indigenous Resistance'. *AlterNative: An International Journal of Indigenous Peoples* 10, no. 3 (2014): 216–31.

Ahmed, Sara. 'Affective Economies'. *Social Text* 22, no. 2 (2004): 117–39.

Ahmed, Sara. 'The Politics of Bad Feeling'. *Australasian Journal of Critical Race and Whiteness Studies* 1 (2005): 72–85.

Ahmed, Sara. 'The Language of Diversity'. *Ethnic and Racial Studies* 30, no. 2 (2007): 235–56.

Ahmed, Sara. 'Multiculturalism and the Promise of Happiness'. *New Formations*, no. 63 (2007): 121–38.

Ahmed, Sara. 'A Phenomenology of Whiteness'. *Feminist Theory* 8, no. 2 (2007): 149–68.

Ahmed, Sara. *On Being Included: Racism and Diversity in Institutional Life*. Durham, NC: Duke University Press, 2012.

Ahmed, Sara. *What's the Use? On the Uses of Use*. Durham, NC: Duke University Press, 2019.

Akbarzadeh, Shahram. 'Investing in Mentoring and Educational Initiatives: The Limits of De-Radicalisation Programmes in Australia'. *Journal of Muslim Minority Affairs* 33, no. 4 (2013): 451–63.

Alfayadh, Fadak. 'Dismantling the Detention Industrial Complex'. In *Incarceration, Migration and Indigenous Sovereignty: Thoughts on Existence and Resistance in Racist Times*, ed. Holly Randell-Moon. Dunedin: Space, Race, Bodies; Department of Media, Film & Communication, University of Otago, 2017, 23–5.

Alfred, Taiaiake and Jeff Corntassel. 'Being Indigenous: Resurgences against Contemporary Colonialism'. *Government and Opposition* 40, no. 4 (2005): 597–614.

Allam, Lorena, Calla Wahlquist, Nick Evershed and Miles Herbert. 'The 474 Deaths Inside: Tragic Toll of Indigenous Deaths in Custody Revealed'. *Guardian*, 8 April 2021. http://www.theguardian.com/australia-news/2021/apr/09/the-474-deaths-inside-rising-number-of-indigenous-deaths-in-custody-revealed.

Alvaro, Alexandra. 'University of Tasmania's New Subject Aims to "Indigenise" Teaching'. ABC News (Australia), 30 May 2021. https://www.abc.net.au/news/2021–05–31/tas-mon-utas-indigenous-learning-on-country/100176826.

Aly, Anne and David Walker. 'Veiled Threats: Recurrent Cultural Anxieties in Australia'. *Journal of Muslim Minority Affairs* 27, no. 2 (1 August 2007): 203–14.

Amos, Yukari Takimoto. 'Voices of Teacher Candidates of Color on White Race Evasion: "I Worried about My Safety!"' *International Journal of Qualitative Studies in Education* 29, no. 8 (2016): 1002–15.

Anthony, Thalia. '"They Were Treating Me like a Dog": The Colonial Continuum of State Harms against Indigenous Children in Detention in the Northern Territory, Australia'. *State Crime Journal* 7, no. 2 (2018): 251–77.

Anyon, Jean. 'Social Class and the Hidden Curriculum of Work'. *Journal of Education* 162 (1980): 67–92.

Apple, Michael W. *Ideology and Curriculum*. London: Routledge & Kegan Paul, 1979.

Appleby, Gabrielle and Megan Davis. 'The Uluru Statement and the Promises of Truth'. *Australian Historical Studies* 49, no. 4 (2 October 2018): 501–9.

Arora, Avneet. 'Australia Announces Changes to Citizenship Test and English Language Program for Migrants'. *SBS Your Language*. https://www.sbs.com.au/language/english/australia-announces-changes-to-citizenship-test-and-english-language-program-for-migrants.

Atkinson, Wayne. 'The Schools of Human Experience'. In *First Australians*, ed. Rachel Perkins and Marcia Langton. Carlton: The Miegunyah Press, 2010, 185–216.

Attwood, Bain. 'Denial in a Settler Society: The Australian Case'. *History Workshop Journal* 84 (1 October 2017): 24–43.

Attwood, Bain and Andrew Markus. *The Struggle for Aboriginal Rights: A Documentary History*. St Leonards: Allen & Unwin, 1999.

Australian Law Reform Commission. 'Disproportionate Incarceration Rate'. 9 January 2018. https://www.alrc.gov.au/publication/pathways-to-justice-inquiry-into-the-incarceration-rate-of-aboriginal-and-torres-strait-islander-peoples-alrc-report-133/executive-summary-15/disproportionate-incarceration-rate.

Bain, Zara. 'Is There Such a Thing as "White Ignorance" in British Education?' *Ethics and Education* 13, no. 1 (2 January 2018): 4–21. https://www.deadlystory.com/page/culture/history/The_1988_Bicentenary_Protest.

Baldwin, Andrew. 'Whiteness and Futurity: Towards a Research Agenda'. *Progress in Human Geography* 36, no. 2 (2012): 172–87.

Baldwin, Davarian L. *In the Shadow of the Ivory Tower: How Universities Are Plundering Our Cities*. New York: Bold Type Books, 2021.

Bargallie, Debbie. *Unmasking the Racial Contract: Indigenous Voices on Racism in the Australian Public Service*. Canberra: Aboriginal Studies Press, 2020.

Barkham, Patrick. 'Australia Votes on How Tightly to Close the Door'. *Guardian*, 10 November 2001. http://www.theguardian.com/world/2001/nov/10/immigration.uk.

Barton, Greg. 'To Shut Down Far-Right Extremism in Australia, We Must Confront the Ecosystem of Hate'. *The Conversation*, 7 February 2021. http://theconversation.com/to-shut-down-far-right-extremism-in-australia-we-must-confront-the-ecosystem-of-hate-154269.

Behrendt, Larissa. 'Genocide: The Distance between Law and Life'. *Aboriginal History* 25 (2001): 132–47.

Bello, Akil. 'How Test Publishers Are Poised to Profit From Pandemic "Learning Loss"'. *Forbes*, 7 April 2021. https://www.forbes.com/sites/akilbello/2021/04/07/how-test-publishers-are-poised-to-profit-from-pandemic-learning-loss.

Benjamin, Ruha. 'Catching Our Breath: Critical Race STS and the Carceral Imagination'. *Engaging Science, Technology, and Society* 2 (2016): 145–56.

Bennett, Joshua. *Being Property Once Myself: Blackness and the End of Man*. Cambridge, MA: Harvard University Press, 2020.

Berg, Laurie and Bassina Farbenblum. *Wage Theft in Australia: Findings of the National Temporary Migrant Work Survey*. New South Wales: Migrant Worker Justice Initiative, 2017. https://www.mwji.org/survey.

Bernstein, Basil, ed. *Class, Codes and Control, Vol. 2*. London: Routledge and Kegan Paul, 1973.

Bhambra, Gurminder. *Rethinking Modernity Postcolonialism and the Sociological Imagination*. Basingstoke: Palgrave Macmillan, 2007.

Bhambra, Gurminder. *Connected Sociologies*. London: Bloomsbury Publishing, 2014.

Bhandar, Brenna. *Colonial Lives of Property*. Durham, NC: Duke University Press, 2018.

Bhattacharyya, Gargi. *Rethinking Racial Capitalism: Questions of Reproduction and Survival*. London: Rowman & Littlefield, 2018.

Bhattacharya, Tithi, ed. *Social Reproduction Theory: Remapping Class, Recentering Oppression*. London: Pluto Press, 2017.

Birch, Kean and Fabian Muniesa. *Assetization: Turning Things into Assets in Technoscientific Capitalism*. Cambridge, MA: MIT Press, 2020.

Birtles, Bill. 'China Cautions Students about "Racist Incidents" During Coronavirus Pandemic If They Return to Australia'. ABC News (Australia), 9 June 2020. https://www.abc.net.au/news/2020-06-09/china-warns-students-not-to-return-to-australia-after-coronaviru/12337044.

Bishop, Michelle. 'A Rationale for the Urgency of Indigenous Education Sovereignty: Enough's Enough'. *The Australian Educational Researcher* 48, no. 3 (1 July 2021): 419–32.

Black Curriculum, The. https://theblackcurriculum.com.

Blagg, Harry and Thalia Anthony. '"Stone Walls Do Not a Prison Make": Bare Life and the Carceral Archipelago in Colonial and Postcolonial Societies'. In *Human Rights and Incarceration: Critical Explorations*, ed. Elizabeth Stanley. Cham: Springer International Publishing, 2018, 257–83.

Bleiker, Roland, David Campbell, Emma Hutchison and Xzarina Nicholson. 'The Visual Dehumanisation of Refugees'. *Australian Journal of Political Science* 48, no. 4 (2013): 398–416.

Boler, Megan. *Feeling Power: Emotions and Education*. London: Routledge, 1999.

Boochani, Behrouz. *No Friend But the Mountains: Writing from Manus Prison*. Sydney: Pan Macmillan Australia, 2018.

Bowles, Samuel and Herbert Gintis. *Schooling in Capitalist America: Educational Reform and the Contradictions of Economic Life*. New York: Basic Books, 1976.

Bunda, Tracey, Lew Zipin and Marie Brennan. 'Negotiating University "Equity" from Indigenous Standpoints: A Shaky Bridge'. *International Journal of Inclusive Education* 16, no. 9 (2012): 941–57.

Byrd, Jodi A., Alyosha Goldstein, Jodi Melamed and Chandan Reddy. 'Predatory Value: Economies of Dispossession and Disturbed Relationalities'. *Social Text* 36, no. 2 (2018): 1–18.

Cacho, Lisa Marie. *Social Death: Racialized Rightlessness and the Criminalization of the Unprotected*. New York: New York University Press, 2012.

Carey, Jane. '"Wanted! A Real White Australia": The Women's Movement, Whiteness and the Settler Colonial Project, 1900–1940'. In *Studies in Settler Colonialism*, ed. Fiona Bateman and Lionel Pilkington. London: Springer, 2011, 122–39.

Carey, Melissa, and Adam Cunningham. '"Invasion Day" Rally Organiser Says Her Comments Australia Should "Burn to the Ground" Should Not Be Taken Literally'. *The Age*, 26 January 2018. https://www.theage.com.au/national/victoria/invasion-day-rally-organiser-says-her-comments-australia-should-burn-to-the-ground-should-not-be-taken-literally-20180126-p4yyxo.html.

Cargo Classroom. https://cargomovement.org/classroom.

Casinader, Niranjan Robert and Lucas Walsh. 'Teacher Transculturalism and Cultural Difference: Addressing Racism in Australian Schools'. *International Education Journal: Comparative Perspectives* 14, no. 2 (2015): 51–62.

Centre for Indigenous Global Futures, Macquarie University. https://www.mq.edu.au/research/research-centres-groups-and-facilities/resilient-societies/centres/forum-for-indigenous-research-excellence.

Chesterman, John and Brian Galligan. *Citizens without Rights: Aborigines and Australian Citizenship*. Cambridge: Cambridge University Press, 1997.

Chiu, Osmond. 'Eliminating Racism: Or As We Call It, Harmony'. *Meanjin*, 20 March 2019. https://meanjin.com.au/blog/eliminating-racism-or-as-we-call-it-harmony.

Choudry, Aziz. *Learning Activism: The Intellectual Life of Contemporary Social Movements*. Toronto: University of Toronto Press, 2015.

Christian, Michelle. 'A Global Critical Race and Racism Framework: Racial Entanglements and Deep and Malleable Whiteness'. *Sociology of Race and Ethnicity* 5, no. 2 (2019): 169–85.

Chrysanthos, Natassia. 'Inner West School to Spend Millions on Public Park Upgrade under Council Deal'. *Sydney Morning Herald*, 7 May 2020. https://www.smh.com.au/national/nsw/inner-west-school-to-spend-millions-on-public-park-upgrade-under-council-deal-20200504-p54ppe.html.

Chun, Matt. 'Enduring Silence: Anzac Day and the Frontier Wars'. *Overland Literary Journal*, 3 May 2018. https://overland.org.au/2018/05/enduring-silence-anzac-day-and-the-frontier-wars.

Clark, Jennifer. *Aborigines & Activism: Race, Aborigines and the Coming of the Sixties to Australia*. Crawley: University of Western Australia Press, 2008.

Cochrane, Peter. *Best We Forget: The War for White Australia, 1914–18*. Melbourne: Text Publishing, 2018.

Commonwealth of Australia. *Bringing Them Home: Report of the National Inquiry into the Separation of Aboriginal and Torres Strait Islander Children from Their Families*. Sydney: Human Rights and Equal Opportunity Commission, 1997.

Commonwealth of Australia. 'National Framework for Values Education in Australian Schools'. Department of Communications, Information Technology and the Arts, 2005. http://www.curriculum.edu.au/verve/_resources/Framework_PDF_version_for_the_web.pdf.

Compagnoni, Melissa. 'Servant or Slave: Reshaping Australian History through a New Lens'. *SBS Your Language*. 9 December 2016. https://www.sbs.com.au/language/english/servant-or-slave-reshaping-australian-history-through-a-new-lens.

Connell, Raewyn. *Southern Theory: The Global Dynamics of Knowledge in Social Science*. Cambridge: Polity, 2007.

Connell, Raewyn, Gary Dowsett and Sandra Kessler. *Making the Difference: Schools, Families and Social Division*. Sydney: George Allen & Unwin, 1982.

Coram, Stella and Chris Hallinan. 'Critical Race Theory and the Orthodoxy of Race Neutrality: Examining the Denigration of Adam Goodes'. *Australian Aboriginal Studies*, no. 1 (2017).

Croucher, Gwilym and James Waghorne. *Australian Universities: A History of Common Cause*. Sydney: New South Publishing, 2020.

Curthoys, Ann and Clive Moore. 'Working for the White People: An Historiographic Essay on Aboriginal and Torres Strait Islander Labour'. *Labour History*, no. 69 (1995): 1–29.

Dabashi, Hamid. 'Black Lives Matter and Palestine: A Historic Alliance'. Al Jazeera, 6 September 2016. https://www.aljazeera.com/opinions/2016/9/6/black-lives-matter-and-palestine-a-historic-alliance.

d'Abrera, Bella. 'University Audit Finds Humanities Riddled With Critical Race Theory And Identity Politics'. Institute of Public Affairs, 16 January 2021. https://ipa.org.au/ipa-today/university-audit-finds-humanities-riddled-with-critical-race-theory-and-identity-politics.

Davis, Megan. 'The Long Road to Uluru: Walking Together: Truth before Justice'. *Griffith Review*, no. 60 (2018).

Deadly Story. 'The 1988 Bicentenary Protest'. https://www.deadlystory.com/page/culture/history/The_1988_Bicentenary_Protest.

Dhillon, Jaskiran K. 'Indigenous Girls and the Violence of Settler Colonial Policing'. *Decolonization: Indigeneity, Education & Society* 4, no. 2 (17 December 2015): 1–31.

Donda, Leia Maia. 'Why Won't UCL Treat Us Cleaners like Its Other Staff?' *Guardian*, 4 December 2019. http://www.theguardian.com/commentisfree/2019/dec/04/ucl-cleaners-strike-outsourced-staff.

Donnelly, Kevin. *How Political Correctness Is Destroying Australia: Enemies within and Without*. Melbourne: Wilkinson Publishing, 2018.

Du Bois, W.E.B. *Darkwater: Voices from within the Veil*, New York: Harcourt, Brace and Howe, 1920.

Du Bois, W.E.B. *The Souls of Black Folk*. [1903] Oxford: Oxford University Press, 2007.

Du Bois, W.E.B. 'The Souls of White Folk'. *The Independent* (USA), 10 August 1910, reprinted in W.E.B. Du Bois, *Writings*, New York: Library of America, 1987.

Duffy, Conor. '"Brandzac Day": Historian Criticises "New Low in the Commercialisation of Anzac"'. ABC News (Australia), 15 April 2015. https://www.abc.net.au/news/2015–04–15/critics-disgusted-by-vulgar-commercialisation-of-anzac-day/6395756.

Erakat, Noura. 'Whiteness as Property in Israel: Revival, Rehabilitation, and Removal'. *Harvard Journal on Racial & Ethnic Justice* 69 (5 July 2015): 1–36.

Facer, Keri. 'Futures in Education: Towards an Ethical Practice'. Paper commissioned for the UNESCO Futures of Education (2021). https://unesdoc.unesco.org/ark:/48223/pf0000375792.locale=en.

Fanon, Frantz. *The Wretched of the Earth*. [1961] Harmondsworth: Penguin Books., 1969.

Foley, Gary. *A Short History of the Australian Indigenous Resistance 1950–1990*. Vancouver: Subversion Press, 2010.

Free, Cathy. 'Portraits on Campus Lacked Diversity, So This Artist Painted the Blue-Collar Workers Who "Really Run Things"'. *Washington Post*. 24 January 2020. https://www.washingtonpost.

com/lifestyle/2020/01/24/portraits-campus-lacked-diversity-so-this-artist-painted-blue-collar-workers-who-really-run-things.

Frydenberg, Josh. 'Treasurer Josh Frydenberg's 2019 Budget Speech – In Full'. *Guardian*, 2 April 2019. http://www.theguardian.com/australia-news/2019/apr/02/treasurer-josh-frydenbergs-2019-budget-speech-in-full.

Gardiner, John, David Evans and Kenneth Howell. 'Suspension and Exclusion Rates for Aboriginal Students in Western Australia'. *Aboriginal Child at School* 23, no. 1 (1995).

Garma Festival's Youth Forum. 'The Imagination Declaration of the Youth Forum Read at Garma 2019'. NITV, 5 August 2019. https://www.sbs.com.au/nitv/nitv-news/article/2019/08/05/imagination-declaration-youth-forum-read-garma-2019.

Gatwiri, Kathomi and Leticia Anderson. 'The Senate Has Voted to Reject Critical Race Theory from the National Curriculum. What Is It, and Why Does It Matter?' *The Conversation*, 22 June 2021. http://theconversation.com/the-senate-has-voted-to-reject-critical-race-theory-from-the-national-curriculum-what-is-it-and-why-does-it-matter-163102.

Gerrard, Jessica. 'Whose Public, Which Public? The Challenge for Public Education'. *Critical Studies in Education* 59, no. 2 (2018): 1–14.

Gerrard, Jessica, Arathi Sriprakash and Sophie Rudolph. 'Education and Racial Capitalism'. *Race, Ethnicity and Education* (2021). https://doi.org/10.1080/13613324.2021.2001449.

Gerrard, Jessica and Rosie Barron. 'Cleaning Public Education: The Privatisation of School Maintenance Work'. *Journal of Educational Administration and History* 52, no. 1 (2020): 9–21.

Gesturing Towards Decolonial Futures. https://decolonialfutures.net.

Gillborn, David. 'Softly, Softly: Genetics, Intelligence and the Hidden Racism of the New Geneism'. *Journal of Education Policy* 31, no. 4 (2016): 365–88.

Gilmore, Jane. 'Hysteria over Yassmin Abdel-Magied's Anzac Day Post Cannot Be Separated from Racism'. *Sydney Morning Herald*, 27 April 2017 (updated 28 April 2017). https://www.smh.com.au/lifestyle/hysteria-over-yassmin-abdelmagieds-anzac-day-post-cannot-be-separated-from-racism-20170427-gvtjdj.html.

Gilmore, Ruth Wilson. *Golden Gulag: Prisons, Surplus, Crisis, and Opposition in Globalizing California*. Berkeley: University of California Press, 2007.

Gilroy, Paul. *Postcolonial Melancholia*. New York: Columbia University Press, 2005.

Gipson, G. 'Creating and Imagining Black Futures through Afrofuturism'. In *#identity: Hashtagging Race, Gender, Sexuality, and Nation*, ed. A. De Kosnik and K. Feldman. Ann Arbor: University of Michigan Press, 2019, 84–103.

Givens, Jarvis R. *Fugitive Pedagogy: Carter G. Woodson and the Art of Black Teaching*. Cambridge, MA: Harvard University Press, 2021.

Goldberg, David Theo. *The Racial State*. Malden, MA: Blackwell Publishers, 2002.

Golding, David and Kyle Kopsick. 'The Colonial Legacy in Cambridge Assessment Literature Syllabi'. *Curriculum Perspectives* 39, no. 1 (2019): 7–17.

Goldstein, Dana. 'Does It Hurt Children to Measure Pandemic Learning Loss?'. *New York Times*, 8 April 2021. https://www.nytimes.com/2021/04/08/us/school-testing-education-covid.html.

Gould, Eliga H. 'Entangled Histories, Entangled Worlds: The English-Speaking Atlantic as a Spanish Periphery'. *The American Historical Review* 112, no. 3 (2007): 764–86.

Government of Canada, Royal Canadian Mounted Police. 'Missing and Murdered Aboriginal Women: A National Operational Overview'. 27 May 2014. https://www.rcmp-grc.gc.ca/en/missing-and-murdered-aboriginal-women-national-operational-overview.

Graham, Linda J., Tony McCarthy, Callula Killingly, Haley Tancredi and Shiralee Poed. 'Inquiry into Suspension, Exclusion and Expulsion Processes in South Australian Government Schools: Final Report'. Brisbane: The Centre for Inclusive Education, QUT, 2020.

Grollman, Eric Anthony. 'Invisible Labor: Exploitation of Scholars of Color in Academia'. *Conditionally Accepted: A Space for Scholars on the Margins of Academia* 15 (2015).

Gross, Matthias and Linsey McGoey. *Routledge International Handbook of Ignorance Studies*. London: Routledge, 2015.

Gulmanelli, Stefano. 'John Howard and the "Anglospherist" Reshaping of Australia'. *Australian Journal of Political Science* 49, no. 4 (2014): 581–95.

Gutiérrez Rodríguez, Encarnación. 'The Coloniality of Migration and the "Refugee Crisis": On the Asylum-Migration Nexus, the Transatlantic White European Settler Colonialism-Migration and Racial Capitalism'. *Refuge: Canada's Journal on Refugees*, 34, no. 1 (2018): 16–28.

Hage, Ghassan. *White Nation: Fantasies of White Supremacy in a Multicultural Nation*. London: Routledge, 2000.

Hage, Ghassan. *Writings on Nationalism, Multiculturalism and Racism: Including White Nation and against Paranoid Nationalism*. Ultimo: Australian Society of Authors, 2014.

Hage, Ghassan. *Is Racism an Environmental Threat?* Cambridge: Polity, 2017.

Hall, Lisa. '"Not Looking at Us Level": Systemic Barriers Faced by Aboriginal Teachers in Remote Communities in Central Australia'. *Journal of Critical Race Inquiry* 5, no. 1 (2018): 74–101.

Hall, Louise. 'Scott McIntyre Not Sacked for Controversial Anzac Day'. *Sydney Morning Herald*, 17 December 2015. https://www.smh.com.au/business/companies/scott-mcintyre-not-sacked-for-controversial-anzac-day-opinion-sbs-20151217-glpwkt.html.

Hannah, Mark. 'Aboriginal Workers in the Australian Agricultural Company, 1824–1857'. *Labour History* 82 (2002): 17–33.

Hare, Jan, Christine Bridge and Amber Shilling. 'Preparing Teachers through Land Education: Indigenous Erasure, Reclamation, and Resurgence in Campus Spaces'. In *Indigenous Futures and Learnings Taking Place*, ed. Ligia (Licho) López López and Gioconda Coello. London: Routledge, 2020, 138–56.

Harris, Cheryl. 'Whiteness as Property'. *Harvard Law Review* 106, no. 8 (1993): 1707–91.

Hartman, Saidiya V. *Scenes of Subjection: Terror, Slavery, and Self-Making in Nineteenth-Century America*. Oxford: Oxford University Press, 1997.

Hartman, Saidiya V. 'Saidiya Hartman on Insurgent Histories and the Abolitionist Imaginary'. 14 July 2020. https://www.artforum.com/interviews/saidiya-hartman-83579.

Henderson, Anna. 'Prime Minister Tony Abbott Describes Sydney as "Nothing But Bush" Before First Fleet Arrived in 1788'. ABC News (Australia), 14 November 2014. https://www.abc.net.au/news/2014–11–14/abbot-describes-1778-australia-as-nothing-but-bush/5892608.

Henriques-Gomes, Luke. '"Callous Treatment": International Students Stranded in Australia Struggle to Survive'. *Guardian*, 16 September 2020. http://www.theguardian.com/australia-news/2020/sep/17/callous-treatment-international-students-stranded-in-australia-struggle-to-survive.

Higginbotham, Will. 'Blackbirding: Australia's History of Kidnapping Pacific Islanders'. ABC News (Australia), 16 September 2017. https://www.abc.net.au/news/2017–09–17/blackbirding-australias-history-of-kidnapping-pacific-islanders/8860754.

Hirshfield, Laura E. and Tiffany D. Joseph. '"We Need a Woman, We Need a Black Woman": Gender, Race, and Identity Taxation in the Academy'. *Gender and Education* 24, no. 2 (2012): 213–27.

Ho, Christina. 'My School and Others: Segregation and White Flight'. *Australian Review of Public Affairs* 10, no. 1 (2011): 1–2.

Hobbs, Harry. 'Victoria's Truth-telling Commission: To Move Forward, We Need to Answer For the Legacies of Colonisation'. *The Conversation*, 9 March 2021. http://theconversation.com/victorias-truth-telling-commission-to-move-forward-we-need-to-answer-for-the-legacies-of-colonisation-156746.

Hodge, Paul. 'A Grievable Life? The Criminalisation and Securing of Asylum Seeker Bodies in the "Violent Frames" of Australia's Operation Sovereign Borders'. *Geoforum* 58 (2015): 122–31.

Hogarth, Melitta. 'The Power of Words: Bias and Assumptions in the Aboriginal and Torres Strait Islander Education Action Plan'. *The Australian Journal of Indigenous Education* 46, no. 1 (2017): 44–53.

Hokari, Minoru. 'From Wattie Creek to Wattie Creek: An Oral Historical Approach to the Gurindji Walk-Off'. *Aboriginal History* 24 (2000): 98–116.

Holland, Alison. 'Black Lives Matter Has Brought a Global Reckoning with History. This Is Why the Uluru Statement Is So Crucial'. *The Conversation*, 21 December 2020. https://theconversation.com/

black-lives-matter-has-brought-a-global-reckoning-with-history-this-is-why-the-uluru-statement-is-so-crucial-149974.

Hoosan, Dujuan. 'I Am Cheeky, But No Kid Should Be in Jail. This Is Why I Addressed the UN at Just 12 Years Old'. *Guardian*, 11 September 2019. http://www.theguardian.com/commentisfree/2019/sep/12/i-am-cheeky-but-no-kid-should-be-in-jail-this-is-why-i-addressed-the-un-at-just-12-years-old.

Horne, Julia and Geoffrey Sherington. 'Extending the Educational Franchise: The Social Contract of Australia's Public Universities, 1850–1890'. *Paedagogica Historica* 46, no. 1–2 (2010): 207–27.

Howard, John. 'John Howard on Multiculturalism'. Transcript of address by The Prime Minister The Hon John Howard MP, Launch of the National Multicultural Advisory Council's Issues paper *Multicultural Australia: The Way Forward*, Melbourne Town Hall, 11 December 1997. http://www.multiculturalaustralia.gov.au/doc/howard_2.pdf.

Hussein, Shakira, Scheherazade Bloul and Scott Poynting. 'Diasporas and Dystopias on the Beach: Burkini Wars in France and Australia'. In *Islamophobia and the Muslim Student: Disciplining the Intellect*, ed. Irene Zempi and Imran Awan. Abingdon: Routledge, 2019, 263–74.

Ien Ang. 'From White Australia to Fortress Australia: The Anxious Nation in the New Century'. In *Legacies of White Australia: Race, Culture and Nation*, ed. L. Jayasuriya, D. Walker and J. Gothard. Perth: University of Western Australia Press, 2003, 51–70.

Ince, Onur Ulas. *Colonial Capitalism and the Dilemmas of Liberalism*. Oxford: Oxford University Press, 2018.

Initiative for Indigenous Futures. http://indigenousfutures.net.

Jacks, Timna. 'White Flight: Race Segregation in Melbourne State Schools'. *The Age*, 2 May 2016. https://www.theage.com.au/national/victoria/white-flight-race-segregation-in-melbourne-state-schools-20160501-goj516.html.

Jelin, Elizabeth. *State Repression and the Labors of Memory*. Minneapolis: University of Minnesota Press, 2003.

Jessop, Bob. 'Varieties of Academic Capitalism and Entrepreneurial Universities'. *Higher Education* 73, no. 6 (2017): 853–70.

Karmi, Ghada. 'The Conflict in the Middle East Is Sustained By the Silencing of Palestinians'. *Guardian*, 10 June 2021. http://www.

theguardian.com/commentisfree/2021/jun/10/conflict-middle-east-silencing-palestinians-rights.

Kenway, Jane and Johannah Fahey. 'Public Pedagogies and Global Emoscapes'. *Pedagogies: An International Journal* 6, no. 2 (2011): 167–79.

Keynes, Matilda and Beth Marsden, 'Ontology, Sovereignty, Legitimacy: Two Key Moments When History Curriculum Was Challenged in Public Discourse and the Curricular Effects, Australia 1950s and 2000s', *History of Education Review* 50, no. 2 (2021): 130–45.

Khatun, Samia. *Australianama: The South Asian Odyssey in Australia*. Oxford: Oxford University Press, 2018.

Kidd, Rosalind. *The Way We Civilise: Aboriginal Affairs – the Untold Story*. St Lucia: University of Queensland Press, 1997.

Konishi, Shino. 'First Nations Scholars, Settler Colonial Studies, and Indigenous History'. *Australian Historical Studies* 50, no. 3 (3 July 2019): 285–304.

Kundnani, Arun. 'What Is Racial Capitalism?' Arun Kundnani: On Race, Culture, and Empire blog, 23 October 2020. https://www.kundnani.org/what-is-racial-capitalism.

Kwaymullina, Ambelin. *Living on Stolen Land*. Broome: Magabala Books, 2020.

Lake, Marilyn. 'The White Man under Siege: New Histories of Race in the Nineteenth Century and the Advent of White Australia'. *History Workshop Journal* 58, no. 1 (2004): 41–62.

Lake, Marilyn. 'How Do Schoolchildren Learn about the Spirit of Anzac?' In *What's Wrong with ANZAC? The Militarisation of Australian History*, ed. Marilyn Lake, Henry Reynolds, Mark McKenna and Joy Damousi. Sydney: University of NSW Press, 2010, 135–56.

Lake, Marilyn. *Progressive New World: How Settler Colonialism and Transpacific Exchange Shaped American Reform*. Cambridge, MA: Harvard University Press, 2019.

Lake, Marilyn and Henry Reynolds. *Drawing the Global Colour Line: White Men's Countries and the Question of Racial Equality*. Carlton: Melbourne University Publishing, 2008.

Lake, Marilyn, Henry Reynolds, Mark McKenna and Joy Damousi. *What's Wrong with ANZAC? The Militarisation of Australian History*. Sydney: University of NSW Press, 2010.

Le, A.T. 'Support for Doctoral Candidates in Australia During the Pandemic: The Case of the University of Melbourne'. *Studies in Higher Education*, 46 no. 1 (2021): 133–45.

Learn Our Truth. https://learnourtruth.com.

Learn Our Truth. 'Educator Pledge'. https://learnourtruth.com/educator-pledge.

Learn Our Truth. 'Why Are We Not Learning Our Truth?' https://learnourtruth.com/about/#faqs.

Lee, Robert, Tristan Ahtone, Margaret Pearce, Kalen Goodluck, Geoff McGhee, Cody Leff, Katherine Lanpher and Taryn Salinas. 'Land Grab Universities'. *High Country News*. https://www.landgrabu.org.

Lentin, Alana. 'Racism in Public or Public Racism: Doing Anti-Racism in "Post-Racial" Times'. *Ethnic and Racial Studies* 39, no. 1 (2016): 33–48.

Leonardo, Zeus. 'The Color of Supremacy: Beyond the Discourse of "White Privilege"'. *Educational Philosophy and Theory* 36, no. 2 (2004): 137–52.

Lindeman, Tracey. 'Canada: Remains of 215 Children Found at Indigenous Residential School Site'. *Guardian*, 28 May 2021. http://www.theguardian.com/world/2021/may/28/canada-remains-indigenous-children-mass-graves.

Lubiano, Wahneema H., ed. *The House That Race Built: Black Americans, U.S. Terrain*. New York: Pantheon Books, 1997.

Mackey, Eva. *Unsettled Expectations: Uncertainty, Land and Settler Decolonization*. Halifax & Winnipeg: Fernwood Publishing, 2016.

McMillan Cottom, Tressie. 'Where Platform Capitalism and Racial Capitalism Meet: The Sociology of Race and Racism in the Digital Society'. *Sociology of Race and Ethnicity* 6, no. 4 (2020): 441–9.

McNiven, Ian J. and Lynette Russell. *Appropriated Pasts: Indigenous Peoples and the Colonial Culture of Archaeology*. London: Rowman Altamira, 2005.

McQuire, Amy. '"Saving the Children" Are the Three Most Dangerous Words Uttered By White People'. *Guardian*, 14 March 2018. https://www.theguardian.com/commentisfree/2018/mar/14/

saving-the-children-are-the-three-most-dangerous-words-uttered-by-white-people.

Maddison, Sarah. *Beyond White Guilt: The Real Challenge of Black–White Relations in Australia*. Sydney: Allen & Unwin, 2011.

Maddison, Sarah, Tom Clark and Ravi De Costa. *The Limits of Settler Colonial Reconciliation*. Cham: Springer, 2016.

Maldonado-Torres, Nelson. 'On the Coloniality of Being: Contributions to the Development of a Concept'. *Cultural Studies* 21, no. 2–3 (2007): 240–70.

Magoqwana, Babalwa, Qawekazi Maqabuka and Malehoko Tshoaedi. '"Forced to Care" at the Neoliberal University: Invisible Labour as Academic Labour Performed by Black Women Academics in the South African University'. *South African Review of Sociology* 50, no. 3–4 (2019): 6–21.

Marks, Kathy. 'The Anzac Post, Outrage and a Debate about Race'. BBC News, 10 August 2017. https://www.bbc.com/news/world-australia-40712832.

Martin, Francesca. 'Chinese International Students' Wellbeing in Australia: The Road to Recovery'. Report. The University of Melbourne, 9 June 2020. http://minerva-access.unimelb.edu.au/handle/11343/240399.

Martinez, Julia and Claire Lowrie. 'Colonial Constructions of Masculinity: Transforming Aboriginal Australian Men into "Houseboys"'. *Gender & History* 21, no. 2 (2009): 305–23.

Martschenko, Daphne. '"The Train Has Left the Station": The Arrival of the Biosocial Sciences in Education'. *Research in Education* 107, no. 1 (2020): 3–9.

Marx, Karl. *Capital, Vol. 1*. [1867] Chicago: University of Chicago Press, 1952.

Marx, Karl and Friedrich Engels. *The Communist Manifesto* [1848]. London: Vintage, 2010.

Masters, Emma. 'Growing Number of Aboriginal Communities Setting Up Independent Schools to Teach "Both Ways"'. ABC News (Australia), 3 July 2021. https://www.abc.net.au/news/2021-07-04/teaching-blends-aboriginal-culture-language-western-numeracy/100237208.

Matamoros-Fernández, Ariadna. 'Platformed Racism: The Mediation and Circulation of an Australian Race-Based Controversy on Twitter, Facebook and YouTube'. *Information, Communication & Society* 20, no. 6 (2017): 930–46.

May, Dawn. 'The Articulation of the Aboriginal and Capitalist Modes on the North Queensland Pastoral Frontier'. *Journal of Australian Studies* 7, no. 12 (1983): 34–44.

Mayes, Eve. 'Radical Reform and Reforming Radicals in Australian Schooling'. *History of Education Review* 48, no. 2 (2019): 156–70.

Mbembe, Achille. *Critique of Black Reason*. Durham, NC: Duke University Press, 2017.

Mehta, Uday Singh. *Liberalism and Empire: A Study in Nineteenth-Century British Liberal Thought*. Chicago: University of Chicago Press, 2018.

Melamed, Jodi. 'Racial Capitalism'. *Critical Ethnic Studies* 1, no. 1 (2015): 76–85.

Melamed, Jodi. *Represent and Destroy: Rationalizing Violence in the New Racial Capitalism*. Minneapolis: University of Minnesota Press, 2011.

Mignolo, Walter. *Local Histories/Global Designs: Coloniality, Subaltern Knowledges, and Border Thinking*. Princeton: Princeton University Press, 2000.

Millei, Zsuzsa. 'Pedagogy of Nation: A Concept and Method to Research Nationalism in Young Children's Institutional Lives'. *Childhood* 26, no. 1 (2019): 83–97.

Mills, Charles W. *Racial Contract*. Ithaca: Cornell University Press, 1999.

Mills, Charles W. 'White Ignorance'. In *Race and Epistemologies of Ignorance*, ed. Shannon Sullivan and Nancy Tuana. Ithaca: State University of New York Press, 2007, 13–38.

Mills, Charles W. 'White Time: The Chronic Injustice of Ideal Theory 1'. *Du Bois Review* 11, no. 1 (2014): 27–42.

Mills, Charles W. 'Global White Ignorance'. In *Routledge International Handbook of Ignorance Studies*, ed. Matthias Gross and Linsey McGoey. London: Routledge, 2015, 217–27.

Mills, Charles W. *Black Rights/White Wrongs: The Critique of Racial Liberalism*. Oxford: Oxford University Press, 2017.

Molla, Tebeje. 'Refugees and Equity Policy in Australian Higher Education'. *Policy Reviews in Higher Education* 5, no. 1 (2021): 5–27.

Moodie, Nikki. 'Learning about Knowledge: Threshold Concepts for Indigenous Studies in Education'. *The Australian Educational Researcher* 46, no. 5 (1 March 2019): 735–49.

Moore, Robyn. 'Who Is Australian? National Belonging and Exclusion in Australian History Textbooks'. *Review of Education* 9, no. 1 (2021): 55–77.

Moreton-Robinson, Aileen. 'Virtuous Racial States'. *Griffith Law Review* 20, no. 3 (1 January 2011): 641–58.

Moreton-Robinson, Aileen, ed. *Whitening Race: Essays in Social and Cultural Criticism*. Canberra: Aboriginal Studies Press, 2011.

Moreton-Robinson, Aileen. *The White Possessive: Property, Power, and Indigenous Sovereignty*. Minneapolis and London: University of Minnesota Press, 2015.

Moreton-Robinson, Aileen. 'Incommensurable Sovereignties'. In *Routledge Handbook of Critical Indigenous Studies*, ed. Brendan Hokowhitu, Aileen Moreton-Robinson, Linda Tuhiwai-Smith, Chris Andersen and Steve Larkin. Abingdon: Routledge, 2020, 257–68.

Muldoon, Paul. 'A Reconciliation Most Desirable: Shame, Narcissism, Justice and Apology'. *International Political Science Review* 38, no. 2 (2017): 213–26.

Murji, Karim and John Solomos. *Racialization: Studies in Theory and Practice*. Oxford: Oxford University Press, 2005.

Nakata, Martin. 'The Cultural Interface'. *The Australian Journal of Indigenous Education* 36 (2007): 7–14.

Nakata, Martin. *Disciplining the Savages, Savaging the Disciplines*. Canberra: Aboriginal Studies Press, 2007.

Nakata, Martin, Victoria Nakata, Sarah Keech and Reuben Bolt. 'Decolonial Goals and Pedagogies for Indigenous Studies'. *Decolonization: Indigeneity, Education & Society* 1, no. 1 (2012).

National Indigenous Youth Education Coalition. Campaign: Learn Our Truth. https://www.niyec.com/learn-our-truth.

Ndhlovu, Finex. 'Post-Refugee African Australians' Perceptions about Being and Becoming Australian: Language, Discourse and Participation'. *African Identities* 9, no. 4 (2011): 435–53.

Ndlovu-Gatsheni, Sabelo J., ed. *Epistemic Freedom in Africa: Deprovincialization and Decolonization*. London: Routledge, 2018.

Ndlovu-Gatsheni, Sabelo J. '"Moral Evil, Economic Good": Whitewashing the Sins of Colonialism'. Al Jazeera, 26 February 2021. https://www.aljazeera.com/opinions/2021/2/26/colonialism-in-africa-empire-was-not-ethical.

Ngo, Helen. *The Habits of Racism: A Phenomenology of Racism and Racialized Embodiment*. Lanham: Lexington Books, 2017.

Nicoll, Fiona. 'Reconciliation in and out of Perspective: White Knowing, Seeing, Curating and Being at Home in and against Indigenous Sovereignty'. In *Whitening Race: Essays in Social and Cultural Criticism*, ed. A. Moreton-Robinson. Canberra: Aboriginal Studies Press, 2011, 17–31.

Norman, James. 'Why We Are Banning Tourists from Climbing Uluru'. *The Conversation*, 6 November 2017. http://theconversation.com/why-we-are-banning-tourists-from-climbing-uluru-86755.

Ombudsman New South Wales. 'NSW Ombudsman Inquiry into Behaviour Management in Schools: A Special Report to Parliament under s 31 of the Ombudsman Act 1974'. 9 August 2017. https://www.ombo.nsw.gov.au/news-and-publications/publications/reports/community-and-disability-services/nsw-ombudsman-inquiry-into-behaviour-management-in-schools-august-2017.

Omi, Michael and Howard Winant. *Racial Formation in the United States*. [1986] New York: Routledge, 2014.

Ouyang, Yu. 'Australian Invention of Chinese Invasion: A Century of Paranoia, 1888/1988'. *Australian Literary Studies* 17, no. 1 (1995): 74–83.

Pascoe, Bruce. *Dark Emu: Black Seeds Agriculture or Accident?* Broome: Magabala Books, 2014.

Patel, Leigh. 'Desiring Diversity and Backlash: White Property Rights in Higher Education'. *The Urban Review* 47, no. 4 (2015): 657–75.

Patel, Leigh. 'Fugitive Practices: Learning in a Settler Colony'. *Educational Studies* 55, no. 3 (2019): 253–61.

Paulson, Julia, Nelson Abiti, Julian Bermeo Osorio, Carlos Arturo Charria Hernández, Duong Keo, Peter Manning, Lizzi O. Milligan, Kate Moles, Catriona Pennell and Sangar Salih. 'Education as Site of

Memory: Developing a Research Agenda'. *International Studies in Sociology of Education* 29, no. 4 (2020): 429–51.

Pearson, Luke. 'Appropriate Terminology for Aboriginal and Torres Strait Islander People – It's Complicated'. *IndigenousX*, 16 June 2021. https://indigenousx.com.au/appropriate-terminology-for-aboriginal-and-torres-strait-islander-people-its-complicated.

Peterson, Nicolas, Lindy Allen and Louise Hamby. *The Makers and Making of Indigenous Australian Museum Collections*. Melbourne: Melbourne University Publishing, 2008.

Picower, Bree. 'The Unexamined Whiteness of Teaching: How White Teachers Maintain and Enact Dominant Racial Ideologies'. *Race Ethnicity and Education* 12, no. 2 (2009): 197–215.

Porter, Amanda and Eddie Cubillo. 'Not Criminals or Passive Victims: Media Need to Reframe Their Representation of Aboriginal Deaths in Custody'. *The Conversation*, 20 April 2021. http://theconversation.com/not-criminals-or-passive-victims-media-need-to-reframe-their-representation-of-aboriginal-deaths-in-custody-158561.

Potter, Simon J. and Jonathan Saha. 'Global History, Imperial History and Connected Histories of Empire'. *Journal of Colonialism and Colonial History* 16, no. 1 (2015).

Powell, Catherine. 'The Color and Gender of COVID: Essential Workers, Not Disposable People'. Think Global Health blog, 4 June 2020. https://www.thinkglobalhealth.org/article/color-and-gender-covid-essential-workers-not-disposable-people.

Poynting, Scott and Victoria Mason. 'The Resistible Rise of Islamophobia: Anti-Muslim Racism in the UK and Australia Before 11 September 2001'. *Journal of Sociology* 43, no. 1 (2007): 61–86.

Proctor, Helen and Arathi Sriprakash. 'Race and Legitimacy: Historical Formations of Academically Selective Schooling in Australia'. *Journal of Ethnic and Migration Studies* 43, no. 14 (2017): 2378–92.

Pykett, Jessica. 'Citizenship Education and Narratives of Pedagogy'. *Citizenship Studies* 14, no. 6 (1 December 2010): 621–35.

Qi, Jing, Catherine Manathunga, Michael Singh and Tracey Bunda. 'Transcultural and First Nations Doctoral Education and Epistemological Border-Crossing: Histories and Epistemic Justice'. *Teaching in Higher Education* 26, no. 3 (3 April 2021): 340–53.

Queensland Government. 'Study at Queensland Offshore School'. Department of Education International, trading as Education Queensland International. https://eqi.com.au/study-options/study-qld-offshore-school.

Quijano, Aníbal. 'Coloniality and Modernity/Rationality'. *Cultural Studies* 21, no. 2–3 (2007): 168–78.

Ramsay Health Care. 'Former Prime Ministers Launch Ramsay Centre for Western Civilisation'. 8 January 2018. https://www.ramsayhealth.com/News/General-News/Former-Prime-Ministers-launch-Ramsay-Centre-for-Western-Civilisation.

Reid, Teela. '2020: The Year of Reckoning, Not Reconciliation. It's Time to Show Up', *Griffith Review* 67: Matters of Trust (2020). https://www.griffithreview.com/articles/2020-year-of-reckoning.

Riddle, Stewart. 'Australian Curriculum Review: Strengthened But Still a Long Way from an Amazing Curriculum For all Australian Students', *EduResearch Matters*, 3 May 2021. https://www.aare.edu.au/blog/?p=9311

Riemer, Nick. 'Weaponising Learning'. *Sydney Review of Books*, 12 June 2018. https://sydneyreviewofbooks.com/essay/weaponising-learning.

Rizvi, Fazal. 'Children and the Grammar of Popular Racism'. In *Race, Identity and Representation in Education*, ed. Cameron McCarthy, Warren Crichlow, Greg Dimitriadis and Nadine Dolby. New York: Routledge, 2005.

Rizvi, Fazal. 'Multiculturalism in Australia: The Construction and Promotion of an Ideology'. *Journal of Education Policy* 3, no. 4 (1988): 335–50.

Roberts, Dorothy. 'The Ethics of Biosocial Science'. The Tanner Lectures on Human Values. Delivered at Harvard University, 2–3 November 2016.

Robinson, Cedric J. *Black Marxism: The Making of the Black Radical Tradition*. Chapel Hill: University of North Carolina Press, 2000.

Ross, John. 'Living Off the Land: The Universities Reaping the Rewards of Their Locations'. *Times Higher Education*, 24 October 2019. https://www.timeshighereducation.com/features/living-land-universities-reaping-rewards-their-locations.

Rowe, Emma. *Middle-Class School Choice in Urban Spaces: The Economics of Public Schooling and Globalized Education Reform.* Abingdon: Routledge, 2017.

Rowe, Emma. 'Reading Islamophobia in Education Policy through a Lens of Critical Race Theory: A Study of the "Funding Freeze" for Private Islamic Schools in Australia'. *Whiteness and Education* 5, no. 1 (2020): 54–73.

Rudolph, Sophie. 'The Past in the Present: Identifying the Violence of Success and the Relief of Failure'. In *The Relationality of Race in Education Research*, ed. Greg Vass, Jacinta Maxwell, Sophie Rudolph and Kalervo N. Gulson. London: Routledge, 2018, 145–55.

Rudolph, Sophie. *Unsettling the Gap: Race, Politics and Indigenous Education*. New York: Peter Lang, 2019.

Rudolph, Sophie. 'Demanding Dialogue in an Unsettled Settler State: Implications for Education and Justice'. *History of Education Review* 50, no. 2 (2021): 181–95.

Rudolph, Sophie. 'Ngaga-Dji, a Call to Action: Education Justice and Youth Imprisonment'. *The Australian Educational Researcher* 48, no. 3 (1 July 2021): 433–48.

Rudolph, Sophie and Lilly Brown. 'Understanding the Techniques of Colonialism: Indigenous Educational Justice'. In *Powers of Curriculum: Sociological Perspectives on Education*, ed. Brad Gobby and Rebecca Walker. Oxford: Oxford University Press, 2017, 288–320.

Rudolph, Sophie, Arathi Sriprakash and Jessica Gerrard. 'Knowledge and Racial Violence: The Shine and Shadow of "Powerful Knowledge"'. *Ethics and Education* 13, no. 1 (2018): 22–38.

Safi, Michael. 'New Extremism Guidelines Require Schools to Report Suspect Behaviour'. *Guardian*, 4 March 2016. http://www.theguardian.com/australia-news/2016/mar/04/new-extremism-guidelines-require-schools-to-report-suspect-behaviour.

Salter, Peta and Jacinta Maxwell. 'The Inherent Vulnerability of the Australian Curriculum's Cross-Curriculum Priorities'. *Critical Studies in Education* 57, no. 3 (2016): 296–312.

Sardar, Ziauddin. 'Colonizing the Future: The "Other" Dimension of Futures Studies'. *Futures* 25, no. 2 (1993): 179–87.

Schwarz, Bill. *The White Man's World: Memories of Empire*. Oxford: Oxford University Press, 2011.

Scott, Joan Wallach. *In the Name of History*. Budapest and New York: Central European University Press, 2019.

Sentencing Advisory Council. 'Indigenous Young People in Detention'. https://plotly.com/~SAC/375.

Shahjahan, Riyad A. and Kirsten T. Edwards. 'Whiteness as Futurity and Globalization of Higher Education'. *Higher Education* (2021), 1–18. https://doi.org/10.1007/s10734-021-00702-x.

Shotwell, Alexis. *Against Purity: Living Ethically in Compromised Times*. Minneapolis: University of Minnesota Press, 2016.

Siganto, Talissa. '9 yo Refuses to Stand Because Anthem Is For "White People of Australia"'. ABC (Australia), 12 September 2018. https://www.abc.net.au/news/2018-09-12/national-anthem-protest-school-brisbane/10235792.

Silverstein, Ben. 'Reading Sovereignties in the Shadow of Settler Colonialism: Chinese Employment of Aboriginal Labour in the Northern Territory of Australia'. *Postcolonial Studies* 23, no. 1 (2020): 43–57.

Simpson, Audra. *Mohawk Interruptus*. Durham, NC: Duke University Press, 2014.

Slater, Lisa. *Anxieties of Belonging in Settler Colonialism: Australia, Race and Place*. London: Routledge, 2019.

Slattery, Kate. 'Drowning Not Waving: The "Children Overboard" Event and Australia's Fear of the Other'. *Media International Australia* 109, no. 1 (2003): 93–108.

Smith, Andrea. 'Indigeneity, Settler Colonialism, White Supremacy'. In *Racial Formation in the Twenty-First Century*, ed. Daniel Martinez HoSang, Oneka LaBennett and Laura Puildo. Berkeley: University of California Press, 2012, 67–88.

Smith, Bernard. *The Spectre of Truganini*. Sydney: Australian Broadcasting Commission, 1980.

Soufan Center, The. 'White Supremacy Extremism: The Transnational Rise of the Violent White Supremacist Movement'. 27 September 2019. https://thesoufancenter.org/research/white-supremacy-extremism-the-transnational-rise-of-the-violent-white-supremacist-movement.

Sousa Santos, Boaventura de. *Epistemologies of the South: Justice against Epistemicide*. Abingdon: Routledge, 2015.

Sriprakash, Arathi, David Nally, Kevin Myers and Pedro Ramos Pinto. 'Learning with the Past: Racism, Education and Reparative Futures'. Paper commissioned for the UNESCO Futures of Education report (2020). https://unesdoc.unesco.org/ark:/48223/pf0000374045.locale=en.

Sriprakash, Arathi, Peter Sutoris and Kevin Myers. 'The Science of Childhood and the Pedagogy of the State: Postcolonial Development in India, 1950s'. *Journal of Historical Sociology* 32, no. 3 (2019): 345–59.

Sriprakash, Arathi, Leon Tikly and Sharon Walker. 'The Erasures of Racism in Education and International Development: Re-Reading the "Global Learning Crisis"'. *Compare: A Journal of Comparative and International Education* 50, no. 5 (2020): 676–92.

Stein, Sharon. 'A Colonial History of the Higher Education Present: Rethinking Land-Grant Institutions through Processes of Accumulation and Relations of Conquest'. *Critical Studies in Education* 61, no. 2 (2020): 212–28.

Stein, Sharon. 'Navigating Different Theories of Change for Higher Education in Volatile Times'. *Educational Studies* 55, no. 6 (2019): 667–88.

Stein, Sharon, Dallas Hunt, Rene Suša and Vanessa de Oliveira Andreotti. 'The Educational Challenge of Unraveling the Fantasies of Ontological Security'. *Diaspora, Indigenous, and Minority Education* 11, no. 2 (3 April 2017): 69–79.

Stein, Sharon, Vanessa Andreotti, Rene Suša, Sarah Amsler, Dallas Hunt, Cash Ahenakew, Elwood Jimmy, Tereza Cajkova, Will Valley and Camilla Cardoso. 'Gesturing towards Decolonial Futures: Reflections on Our Learnings Thus Far'. *Nordic Journal of Comparative and International Education (NJCIE)* 4, no. 1 (2020): 43–65.

Sukarieh, Mayssoun and Stuart Tannock. 'Subcontracting Academia: Alienation, Exploitation and Disillusionment in the UK Overseas Syrian Refugee Research Industry'. *Antipode* 51, no. 2 (2019): 664–80.

Sullivan, Shannon. 'White World-Traveling'. *The Journal of Speculative Philosophy* 18, no. 4 (2004): 300–4.

Sullivan, Shannon and Nancy Tuana. *Race and Epistemologies of Ignorance*. New York: SUNY Press, 2007.

Sydney Morning Herald. 'Truth Overboard – the Story That Won't Go Away'. 28 February 2006. https://www.smh.com.au/national/truth-overboard-the-story-that-wont-go-away-20060228-gdn224.html.

Tate, John William. 'John Howard's "Nation": Multiculturalism, Citizenship, and Identity'. *Australian Journal of Politics & History* 55, no. 1 (2009): 97–120.

Taylor, Penny Skye and Daphne Habibis. 'Widening the Gap: White Ignorance, Race Relations and the Consequences for Aboriginal People in Australia'. *Australian Journal of Social Issues* 55, no. 3 (2020): 354–71.

Taylor, Sandra and Ravinder Kaur Sidhu. 'Supporting Refugee Students in Schools: What Constitutes Inclusive Education?' *International Journal of Inclusive Education* 16, no. 1 (2012): 39–56.

Taylor, Tony. 'Pyne Curriculum Review Prefers Analysis-free Myth to History'. *The Conversation*, 20 October 2014. http://theconversation.com/pyne-curriculum-review-prefers-analysis-free-myth-to-history-32956.

Thakkar, Sonali. 'Reparative Remembering'. *WSQ: Women's Studies Quarterly* 48, no. 1 (2020): 137–40.

Thomas, Amy Claire. 'Bilingual Education, Aboriginal Self-Determination and Yolngu Control of Shepherdson College, 1972-1983', *History of Education Review* 50, no. 2 (2021): 196–211.

Thomas, Mark. 'Australians Man Your Eskys This January 26'. Picture. https://catalogue.nla.gov.au/Record/4808857?lookfor=author:%22George%20Patterson%20Y%20&%20R%22&offset=3&max=3.

Thomas, Mark. 'Your Country Needs You: BBQ like You've Never BBQ'd Before This Australia Day'. Picture. https://catalogue.nla.gov.au/Record/4808652?lookfor=author:%22George%20Patterson%20Y%20&%20R%22&offset=1&max=3.

Thunig, Amy and Tiffany Jones. '"Don't Make Me Play House-N***er": Indigenous Academic Women Treated as "Black

Performer" within Higher Education'. *The Australian Educational Researcher* 48, no. 3 (1 July 2021): 397–417.

Tilley, Lisa and Robbie Shilliam. *Raced Markets: An Introduction*. Abingdon: Taylor & Francis, 2018.

Tolj, Brianne. 'Aboriginal Activist Calling For Australia to Be "Burnt to the Ground" Slammed as a "Hypocrite" Because She's Paid by Taxpayers'. *Mail Online*, 29 January 2018. http://www.dailymail.co.uk/news/article-5323383/Aboriginal-activist-said-Australia-burn-slammed.html.

Trilling, Daniel. 'Why Is the UK Government Suddenly Targeting "Critical Race Theory"?' *Guardian*, 23 October 2020. http://www.theguardian.com/commentisfree/2020/oct/23/uk-critical-race-theory-trump-conservatives-structural-inequality.

Triple J Hack, 'Education Minister Tells Hack Proposed School History Curriculum Is "Overly Negative" and "Downplaying Western Civilisation"', ABC (Australia), 8 September 2021. https://www.abc.net.au/triplej/programs/hack/education-minister-tells-hack-proposed-school-history-curriculu/13532152.

Tuck, Eve and Rubén A. Gaztambide-Fernández. 'Curriculum, Replacement, and Settler Futurity'. *Journal of Curriculum Theorizing* 29, no. 1 (2013): 72–89.

Tuck, Eve and K. Wayne Yang. 'Decolonization Is Not a Metaphor'. *Decolonization: Indigeneity, Education & Society* 1, no. 1 (2012): 1–40.

Uluru Statement. 'The Uluru Statement from the Heart'. https://ulurustatement.org/the-statement.

United Workers Union. 'ACT School Cleaners Celebrate Success of "Backsourcing" Their Jobs'. 12 February 2020. https://www.unitedworkers.org.au/act-school-cleaners-celebrate-success-of-backsourcing-their-jobs.

Uptin, Jonnell. '"If I Peel off My Black Skin Maybe Then I Integrate". Examining How African-Australian Youth Find Living in a "Post Multicultural" Australia'. *Social Identities* 27, no. 1 (2021): 75–91.

Urban, Rebecca. 2021. 'National Curriculum: Christian Heritage Sacrificed in School Shake-up'. *The Australian*, 29 April 2021. Behind paywall at https://tinyurl.com/ywa23yat.

Van Norden, Bryan W. *Taking Back Philosophy*. New York: Columbia University Press, 2019.

Verán, Cristina. 'Blak Lives Matter: Indigenous Australia's Solidarity with the U.S. Movement for Black Lives'. *Cultural Survival Quarterly Magazine*, September 2020. https://www.culturalsurvival.org/publications/cultural-survival-quarterly/blak-lives-matter-indigenous-australias-solidarity-us.

Verma, Sanmati. 'Kagaz Nahi Dikhayenge / We Won't Show Our Papers'. *Peril Magazine*, no. 42 (24 August 2020). https://peril.com.au/back-editions/edition-42/we-wont-show-our-papers.

Victorian Aboriginal Heritage Council, 'Repatriation of Ceremonial Objects and Human Remains Under the UN Declaration on the Rights of Indigenous Peoples. Submission by the Victorian Aboriginal Heritage Council to the Expert Mechanism on the Rights of Indigenous People'. 24 June 2020. https://www.aboriginalheritagecouncil.vic.gov.au/report-repatriation-ceremonial-objects-and-human-remains-under-un-declaration-rights-indigenous.

Victorian Ombudsman, 'Investigation into Victorian Government School Expulsion'. 14 August 2017. https://www.ombudsman.vic.gov.au/our-impact/investigation-reports/investigation-into-victorian-government-school-expulsions.

Virdee, Satnam. 'Racialized Capitalism: An Account of Its Contested Origins and Consolidation'. *The Sociological Review* 67, no. 1 (2019): 3–27.

Vogl, Anthea and Elyse Methven. 'Life in the Shadow Carceral State: Surveillance and Control of Refugees in Australia'. *International Journal for Crime, Justice and Social Democracy* 9, no. 4: 61–75.

Wahlquist, Calla. 'Indigenous Children in Care Doubled Since Stolen Generations Apology'. *Guardian*, 25 January 2018. http://www.theguardian.com/australia-news/2018/jan/25/indigenous-children-in-care-doubled-since-stolen-generations-apology.

Walker, Sharon. 'Whiteness and Exclusion: An Ethnography of the Racialised Discourse of the UK's Widening Participation Agenda'. Unpublished PhD Thesis, University of Cambridge, 2021.

Walter, Maggie. 'The Voice of Indigenous Data: Beyond the Markers of Disadvantage'. *Griffith Review*, no. 60 (2018): 256–63.

Walton, Jessica, Naomi Priest, Emma Kowal, Fiona White, Brandi Fox and Yin Paradies. 'Whiteness and National Identity: Teacher

Discourses in Australian Primary Schools'. *Race Ethnicity and Education* 21, no. 1 (2018): 132–47.

Watson, Irene. 'Aboriginal Sovereignties: Past, Present and Future (Im) Possibilities'. In *Our Patch: Enacting Australian Sovereignty Post-2001*, ed. Suvendrini Perera. Perth: API Network, 2007, 23–44.

Watts, Rob. 'Beyond Nature and Nurture: Eugenics in Twentieth Century Australian History'. *Australian Journal of Politics & History* 40, no. 3 (1994): 318–34.

Whittaker, Alison. 'So White. So What'. *Meanjin*, Autumn 2020. https://meanjin.com.au/essays/so-white-so-what.

Williams, Lewis, Tracey Bunda, Nick Claxton and Iain MacKinnon. 'A Global De-Colonial Praxis of Sustainability – Undoing Epistemic Violences between Indigenous Peoples and Those No Longer Indigenous to Place'. *The Australian Journal of Indigenous Education* 47, no. 1 (2018): 41–53.

Williamson, Ben. 'Bringing Up the Bio-Datafied Child: Scientific and Ethical Controversies over Computational Biology in Education'. *Ethics and Education* 15, no. 4 (2020): 444–63.

Williamson, Ben. 'Psychodata: Disassembling the Psychological, Economic, and Statistical Infrastructure of "Social-Emotional Learning"'. *Journal of Education Policy* 36, no. 1 (2021): 129–54.

Willis, Paul E. *Learning to Labour: How Working Class Kids Get Working Class Jobs*. Farnborough: Saxon House, 1977.

Wolfe, Patrick. 'Land, Labor, and Difference: Elementary Structures of Race'. *The American Historical Review*, no. 3 (2001): 866–905.

Wolfe, Patrick. 'Settler Colonialism and the Elimination of the Native'. *Journal of Genocide Research* 8, no. 4 (December 2006): 387–409.

Woolford, Andrew and James Gacek. 'Genocidal Carcerality and Indian Residential Schools in Canada'. *Punishment & Society* 18, no. 4 (2016): 400–19.

Young, Michael and Johan Muller. 'On the Powers of Powerful Knowledge'. *Review of Education* 1, no. 3 (2013): 229–50.

Zaglas, Wade. 'IPA Program Director Takes Aim at Anti-racism Program'. *Education Review*, 8 April 2021. https://www-educationreview-com-au.eu1.proxy.openathens.net/2021/04/worse-than-safe-schools-ipa-program-director-takes-aim-at-anti-racism-website.

Index

The Pluto Press Newsletter

Hello friend of Pluto!

Want to stay on top of the best radical books we publish?

Then sign up to be the first to hear about our new books, as well as special events, podcasts and videos.

You'll also get 50% off your first order with us when you sign up.

Come and join us!

Go to bit.ly/PlutoNewsletter

Thanks to our Patreon subscriber:

Ciaran Kane

Who has shown generosity and comradeship in support of our publishing.